Series / Number 07-011

MULTIDIMENSIONAL SCALING

JOSEPH B. KRUSKAL
MYRON WISH

Bell Laboratories
Murray Hill, N.J.

SAGE PUBLICATIONS / Beverly Hills / London

For information address:

SAGE PUBLICATIONS, INC.
275 South Beverly Drive
Beverly Hills, California 90212

SAGE PUBLICATIONS LTD
28 Banner Street
London EC1Y 8QE

International Standard Book Number 0-8039-0940-3

Library of Congress Catalog Card No. L.C. 77-93286

TWELFTH PRINTING, 1986

When citing a University Paper, please use the proper form. Remember to cite the
correct Sage University Paper series title and include the paper number. One of the
two following formats can be adapted (depending on the style manual used):

(1) IVERSEN, GUDMUND R. and NORPOTH, HELMUT (1976) "Analysis of
Variance." Sage University Paper series on Quantitative Applications in the Social
Sciences, 07-001. Beverly Hills and London: Sage Pubns.

OR

(2) Iversen, Gudmund R. and Norpoth, Helmut. 1976. *Analysis of Variance*. Sage
University Paper series on Quantitative Applications in the Social Sciences, series no.
07-001. Beverly Hills and London: Sage Publications.

CONTENTS

Editor's Introduction

MULTIDIMENSIONAL SCALING (or MDS) is a set of mathematical techniques that enable a researcher to uncover the "hidden structure" of data bases, as illustrated below.* The authors, who are among the pioneers in developing and using these techniques, deal very concretely with the problems really faced in using them, and present varied applications.

An example illustrating an interesting MULTIDIMENSIONAL SCALING application in political science involves data from a 1968 election study conducted by the Survey Research Center of the University of Michigan.** Each respondent in a national sample evaluated 12 actual or possible candidates for President of the United States. How similarly did the public view the candidates? What identifiable features can we discern in the varying evaluations of the candidates that can help us understand what led individual citizens to their decisions? MULTIDIMENSIONAL SCALING can help answer these questions by locating the political candidates in a spatial configuration or "map." Once we have located the candidates or points in (multidimensional) space, we seek to determine the hidden structure, or theoretical meaning of this spatial representation of candidates.

Applying MULTIDIMENSIONAL SCALING to these data provides a way of reducing the data about 12 candidates to two dimensions representing the hidden structure of the data (here, partisanship and ideology). By finding key differences between political candidates at opposite ends of each dimension, we can attempt to develop indicators of variables that can be measured in future elections.

---

*See some other papers in this series for discussions of related techniques. Jae-on Kim and Charles Mueller (forthcoming) discuss *Factor Analysis*, which is also concerned with the questions raised by multivariate analysis, and is related to multidimensional scaling. For a related approach to the determination of hidden structures or unmeasured variables, see John L. Sullivan and Stanley Feldman (forthcoming), *Multiple Indicators*. A technique for comparing dimensional structures is discussed by Mark Levine (1977) *Canonical Correlation and Factor Comparison*. Sage University Papers on Quantitative Applications in the Social Sciences, series no. 07-006. Beverly Hills and London: Sage Publications.

**These results are reported in H. F. Weisberg and J. G. Rusk (1970) "Dimensions of candidate evaluation." Amer. Pol. Sci. Rev. 64 (December): 1167-1185.

- Psychologists, who were instrumental in developing the techniques discussed, have used them to understand the perception and evaluation of auditory stimuli (such as speech and musical tones), visual stimuli (such as colors and faces), and social entities (such as personality traits and social situations).

- Sociologists have used these methods to determine the structure of groups and organizations, based on members' perceptions of one another and their interaction patterns.

- Anthropologists have used these methods for comparing different cultural groups, based on their beliefs, language, and artifacts.

- Economists and marketing researchers have used these methods for investigating consumer reactions to a wide variety of product classes.

- Educational researchers have used these methods to study the structure of intelligence, of different test batteries, and of classroom environments.

These are just some of the uses of MULTIDIMENSIONAL SCALING. More examples will be found in the pages that follow, and the techniques can be applied to data gathered in many fields.

—E. M. Uslaner, Series Editor

JOSEPH B. KRUSKAL
MYRON WISH
Bell Laboratories
Murray Hill, N.J.

1. BASIC CONCEPTS OF MULTIDIMENSIONAL SCALING

INTRODUCTION

Suppose you are given a map showing the locations of several cities in the United States, and are asked to construct a table of distances between these cities (see Figures 1A and 1B). It is a simple matter to fill in any entry in the table by measuring the distance between the cities with a ruler, and converting the ruler distance into the real distance by using the scale of the map (e.g., one cm. = 30 kilometers).

Now consider the reverse problem, where you are given the table of distances between the cities, and are asked to produce the map. Geometric procedures are available for this purpose, but considerably more effort would be required. In essence, multidimensional scaling, or MDS, is a method for solving this reverse problem (see Figure 1C). The typical application of MDS, however, is much more complicated than this simple example would suggest. For one thing, the data usually contain considerable error, or "noise." For another, it is seldom known in advance whether a simple two-dimensional map will be adequate, or whether a "map" using three, or four, or even more dimensions is needed.

Multidimensional scaling, then, refers to a class of techniques. These techniques use *proximities* among any kind of objects as input. A proximity is a number which indicates how similar or how different two objects are, or are perceived to be, or any measure of this kind. The chief output is a spatial representation, consisting of a geometric *configuration of points,* as on a map. Each point in the configuration corresponds to one of the objects. This configuration reflects the "hidden structure" in the data, and often makes the data much easier to comprehend. By reflecting the data structure we mean that the larger the dissimilarity (or the smaller the similarity) between the two objects, as shown by their proximity value, the further apart they should be in the spatial map. We note that MDS is sometimes used indirectly to analyze data which are not proximities, by forming proximities as an intermediate step.

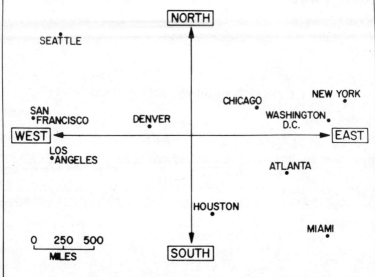

(A) GEOGRAPHIC LOCATIONS OF TEN U.S. CITIES

CITIES	ATLA.	CHIC.	DENV.	HOUS.	L.A.	MIAMI	N.Y.	S.F.	SEAT.	WASH D.C.
ATLANTA		587	1212	701	1936	604	748	2139	2182	543
CHICAGO	587		920	940	1745	1188	713	1858	1737	597
DENVER	1212	920		879	831	1726	1631	949	1021	1494
HOUSTON	701	940	879		1374	968	1420	1645	1891	1220
LOS ANGELES	1936	1745	831	1374		2339	2451	347	959	2300
MIAMI	604	1188	1726	968	2339		1092	2594	2734	923
NEW YORK	748	713	1631	1420	2451	1092		2571	2408	205
SAN FRANCISCO	2139	1858	949	1645	347	2594	2571		678	2442
SEATTLE	2182	1737	1021	1891	959	2734	2408	678		2329
WASHINGTON D.C.	543	597	1494	1220	2300	923	205	2442	2329	

(B) AIRLINE DISTANCES BETWEEN TEN U.S. CITIES

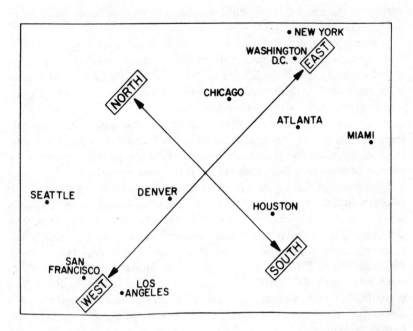

(C) CONFIGURATION OBTAINED BY APPLYING MULTIDIMENSIONAL SCALING
TO THE AIRLINE DISTANCES

Figure 1: The Basic Concept of Multidimensional Scaling

When multidimensional scaling yields useful insights, these generally result from examining the configuration. One of the most important methods of examination is simply to look at the arrangement of points, where each point has been labelled to indicate which object it represents. There are systematic methods, however, which are sometimes used to supplement this direct examination. Before going into detail about the methods of analysis and interpretation, we shall briefly describe some procedures that can be used to obtain proximities data. More extensive discussions of data collection methods can be found in Coombs (1964), Shepard (1972), and Wish (1972).

SOME METHODS FOR OBTAINING PROXIMITIES DATA

A common procedure for obtaining proximities data is to ask people to directly judge the "psychological distance" (or closeness) of the stimulus objects. Although "similarity" and "dissimilarity" are most frequently used to elicit the proximity judgements, alternative words are relatedness, dependence, association, complementarity, substitutability, and so on. In order to discover rather than impose the dimensions, the attributes on which the stimuli are to be judged are usually not specified. Subjects can, however, be asked for specific kinds of similarity, for example, political similarity or cultural similarity of nations.

A simple method useful for relatively large stimulus sets (say about 50 to 100 objects) is to have subjects sort, or cluster, the stimuli according to perceived similarity (see Rosenberg et al., 1968). The typical instructions are to place the stimuli into mutually exclusive and exhaustive categories so that stimuli in the same category are more similar to each other than to those in other categories. (There are modifications of this sorting procedure that have some advantages; see Rosenberg and Kim, 1975, and Wish, 1976.) A matrix of proximities among objects can be derived for the group by counting the number of times each pair of stimuli is put in the same category.

Stimulus confusability is a measure of proximity arising in certain kinds of psychological experiments. Stimulus-stimulus confusions occur in tasks in which subjects judge whether two stimuli presented to them are the same or different. The percentage of "same" responses to a pair of physically different stimuli is the measure of confusability for the two stimuli (see Shepard, 1963, and Wish, 1967). Stimulus-response confusions occur in tasks where subjects attempt to identify the single stimulus presented to them. The percentage of times subjects respond "j" when stimulus i is presented is a measure of stimulus-response confusability (see Shepard, 1974, and Wish and Carroll, 1974).

The amount of communication and interaction between individuals, groups, or other entities can be regarded as a measure of their proximity. An MDS analysis of such data provides a sociometric map in which greater distance reflects less interaction between the associated entities (see Jones and Young, 1972). Likewise a map of communication or information flow between cities or other units can be determined from an MDS analysis of telephone traffic, travel volume, or amount of other transactions from one city to all others (see Slater, 1976, and Coombs, 1964). Such data may need to be "processed" before the MDS analysis to remove the effect of city size from the data.

A very common way to get proximities from data that are not proximities and hence inappropriate for MDS in their original form is to compute some measure of profile similarity or dissimilarity between rows (or columns) of a table. (It is sometimes useful to apply the same procedures to a matrix of proximities, thereby obtaining a new matrix of derived proximities.) For example, the rows of the original table could correspond to various nations, and the columns could be such measures as gross national product, energy consumption, or number of political parties. The most common ways to derive a profile proximity measure are to compute correlations between variables or squared distances between the stimuli (Wish and Carroll, 1974). While correlations have usally been analyzed by factor analysis and related procedures (see Banks and Gregg, 1965; Rummel, 1969; and Sawyer, 1967), they can also be regarded as proximities and analyzed by MDS (see Guttman, 1966; Weisberg and Rusk, 1970).

An Application of MDS to Morse Code Confusions Data

Figure 2 consists of confusions among 36 auditory Morse code signals, which were collected by Rothkopf (1957). Each signal consists of a sequence of dots and dashes, such as $-\cdot-$ for K and $\cdot\cdot---$ for 2. Subjects who did not know Morse code listened to a pair of signals (produced at a fixed rapid rate by machine and separated by a quiet period of 1.4 seconds), and were required to state whether the two signals they heard were the same or different. Each number in the table is the percentage of roughly 150 observers

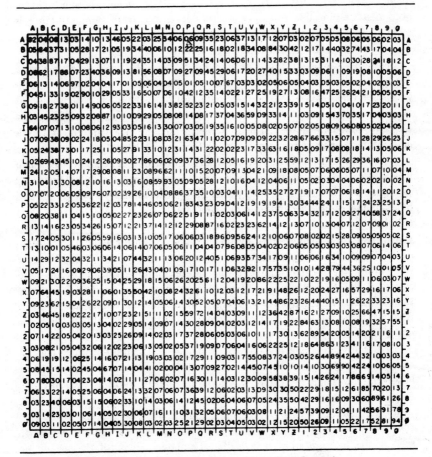

Figure 2: Rothkopf's Data on Similarities Among Morse Code Symbols

who responded "same" to the row signal followed by the column signal. Notice that the conventional Morse code *letter names* for the signals do not enter into the experiment in any way, and are used in the table simply as convenient names.

The diagonal of the table corresponds to pairs which are truly the same, so we expect the diagonal entries to be large: the smallest one is 84%, corresponding to the pair BB. Off-diagonal entries correspond to pairs which are truly different, so we expect these entries to be smaller: in fact, many of them are below 10%. The largest off-diagonal entry is 84% (corresponding to BX, $-\cdots$ $-\cdots-$).

This matrix is roughly symmetric. That is, if we consider corresponding entries above and below the diagonal, like BX and XB, then usually one is large if the other is large, and one is small if the other is small. Applications of MDS always require matrices which are at least roughly symmetric. (We note that despite this rough symmetry, deviations from symmetry in this table are highly significant statistically, and follow some interesting patterns. This does not involve any logical contradiction.)

Figure 3A shows the result of applying MDS to the proximities in Figure 2. (This application is essentially taken from Shepard, 1963, who also analyzes three other sets of Morse code data.) MDS just yields a configuration of 36 points. These points are at the centers of the circles. To this configuration we have added the letters, for convenience in reference, and the dot-dash description of the auditory signals which the subjects heard.

In this application the proximities are similarities, that is, a large value means that the two signals are very much alike. Consider two signals, for example, B $-\cdots$ and X $-\cdots-$, which have large similarity values, 84% and 64%. In the geometric configuration the points for B and X are very close together. Likewise consider two signals, for example E $\cdot$ and 0 $-----$, which have very small similarity values, 3% and 5%. In the geometric configuration the points for E and 0 are very far apart. For other signals, the same thing holds true: a large similarity value corresponds to a small distance, and a small similarity value corresponds to a large distance. Despite a few exceptions, there is a clear relationship which we display more fully later. This is what we mean by saying that the geometric configuration reflects the proximity values.

MDS is a systematic procedure for obtaining a configuration which has this relationship to the proximity data. Once the configuration has been obtained, however, it is usually important to interpret it. Before looking at the interpretation which Shepard gave to this diagram, we strongly advise finding one's own interpretation. The process of interpreting the configuration is the central step in many applications, and is best learned by active participation. In seeking the interpretation, recall that the letter names for the signals are

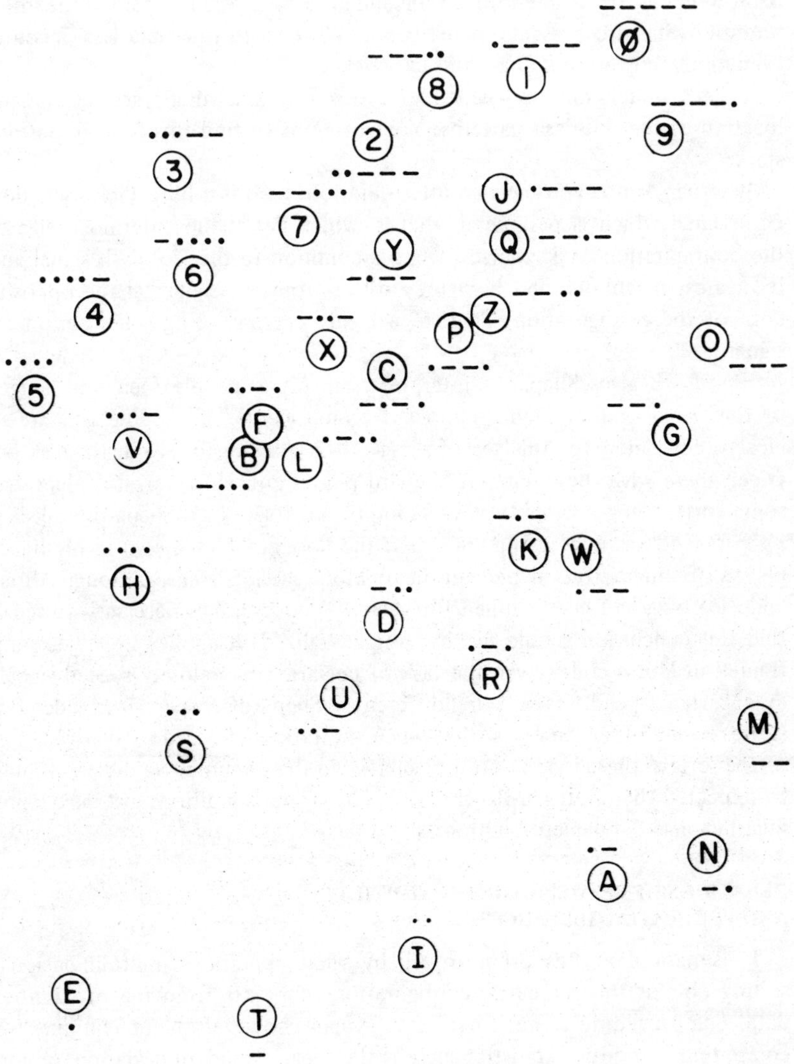

Figure 3A: Configuration Resulting from Morse Code Similarities

completely irrelevant. Thus an interpretation means some systematic relationship between the dot-dash pattern and location in the configuration.

One of the authors has on several occasions asked large audiences to seek their own interpretation, indicating success by raised hands. Typically, in 30 or 40 seconds about one-third of the audience obtains all or part of the interpretation Shepard presents in his paper. With more time and less pressure, even more people should have this experience.

Take as much time as needed, and look for something systematic in the location of the dot-dash patterns. Your attempt to find this is an important step!

Whether or not you have an interpretation, here is a hint. Pick some dot-dash signal which is peripheral, that is, which lies at the outermost edge of the configuration. Ask yourself what is common to this dot-dash signal and its nearest neighbors, and how they differ from the signals at the opposite edge of the configuration. Then repeat this process, using other peripheral signals.

Figure 3B gives Shepard's interpretation. Many people focus on "length of the signal" rather than "number of components." Since the two are so closely correlated for this set of signals, it is not possible to distinguish between them with these data, as Shepard points out. However, it is plain that some sort of length variable plays an important role. When Shepard published his paper, it was new information that the two variables shown in his figure play a dominant role in perception of Morse code signals, although Morse code learning had been studied for years. Of course, it is necessary to recall that this conclusion should not be overgeneralized: it applies to subjects untrained in Morse code, given the task of declaring two closely spaced signals at a certain speed "same" or "different." Shepard's paper clearly demonstrates, using other data sets, that when the task is changed to identification of the letters, there is an interesting change in the dominant variables. It must be expected that a substantial change in any of the conditions just mentioned might change the perception process.

RELATIONSHIP BETWEEN THE PROXIMITIES AND THE SPATIAL DISTANCES

It is natural at this point to ask by what operations multidimensional scaling obtains the geometric configuration of points from the proximities data. The procedure is much harder to explain, however, than techniques for computing descriptive statistics such as the mean, standard deviation, or correlation coefficient, or for plotting geometric diagrams such as histograms and scatter plots. Even for methods of data analysis as complicated as the analysis of variance and linear regression, the actual operations necessary for simple versions can be presented without too much difficulty.

Multidimensional scaling calculations are much more complex, and even the simplest versions are virtually never performed without the aid of a computer. Furthermore, a surprising variety of different computational methods are used which on the surface bear little resemblance to one another. An actual description of the computational procedures used is outside the scope of this paper. We will give a descriptive analogy for one major computational method, but even this must be deferred until after a considerable detour. A full description of the same computational procedure may be found in Kruskal (1976).

Mathematically, it is possible to carry out MDS not only in two-dimensional space (the plane) and three-dimensional space, but also in R-dimensional space for R = 1,2,3,4, etc. While four-dimensional space is impossible to visualize in the ordinary sense, there are numerous ways to represent it visually (although imperfectly), and there is no difficulty in dealing with it mathematically. The same holds true for five, six, and R-dimensional space with one important proviso: the larger the value of R, the more imperfect are the various graphical devices for displaying the results.

NOTATION AND TERMINOLOGY

Before proceeding further we must define some notation and terminology. The data pertain to some collection of objects; they could be faces, colors, countries, political candidates, or stimuli of any kind (real or conceptual). We shall index the objects primarily by the letter i and secondarily by j, and we shall suppose that i and j run from 1 to I if there are I objects. (Frequently we find it convenient to use a small letter for an index, and the corresponding capital letter to indicate the number of different values this index can have.) The proximity or data value connecting object i with object j we represent by δ_{ij}. We arrange the values δ_{ij} in a matrix which we call Δ. For example, if $I = 4$,

$$\Delta = \begin{bmatrix} \delta_{11} & \delta_{12} & \delta_{13} & \delta_{14} \\ \delta_{21} & \delta_{22} & \delta_{23} & \delta_{24} \\ \delta_{31} & \delta_{32} & \delta_{33} & \delta_{34} \\ \delta_{41} & \delta_{42} & \delta_{43} & \delta_{44} \end{bmatrix}.$$

In many situations there may be no effective difference in meaning between δ_{ij} and δ_{ji}, and there may be no meaning at all for δ_{ii}, so that the data values may not form an entire matrix, but only part of one. Also, in some situations we may have repeated measurements for the same proximity, so that a single cell in the matrix corresponds to several distinct data values. For the moment, however, it will be simpler to assume that the data constitute an ordinary complete matrix as shown here.

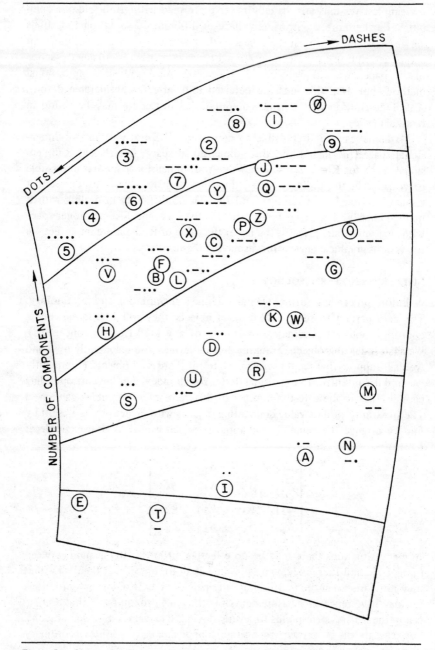

Figure 3B: Shepard's Interpretation of Morse Code Configuration

Each object is represented by a point. We use x_i to indicate the point which corresponds to the ith object, as shown in Figure 4A. We use X to indicate the entire configuration of points $x_1, \ldots, x_I$. By using a coordinate system, each point can be represented by coordinates, as shown in Figure 4B. For two-dimensional space we write the coordinates of x_i as (x_{i1}, x_{i2}). For R-dimensional space we write

$$x_1 = (x_{11}, \ldots, x_{1r}, \ldots, x_{1R})$$

$$\cdot$$
$$\cdot$$
$$\cdot$$

$$x_i = (x_{i1}, \ldots, x_{ir}, \ldots, x_{iR})$$

$$\cdot$$
$$\cdot$$
$$\cdot$$

$$x_I = (x_{I1}, \ldots, x_{Ir}, \ldots, x_{IR}).$$

Strictly speaking, a point is a geometrical object and is distinct from the sequence of coordinates which represents it. However, we shall follow the common custom of talking as if the point were the same thing as its R-tuple of coordinates.

The distance between the points of X play a central role in MDS. We indicate the distance between two points x_i and x_j by

$$d(x_i, x_j) = \text{distance from } x_i \text{ to } x_j,$$

and we frequently simplify this to d_{ij},

$$d_{ij} = d(x_i, x_j).$$

Unless otherwise indicated, distance always mean ordinary Euclidean distance, which we can measure with a ruler on the configuration. It is well-known that this distance can be calculated by the Pythagorean formula, namely,

$$d_{ij} = \sqrt{(x_{i1} - x_{j1})^2 + \ldots + (x_{iR} - x_{jR})^2},$$

which can be written more briefly by using a summation sign to indicate the sum of many terms,

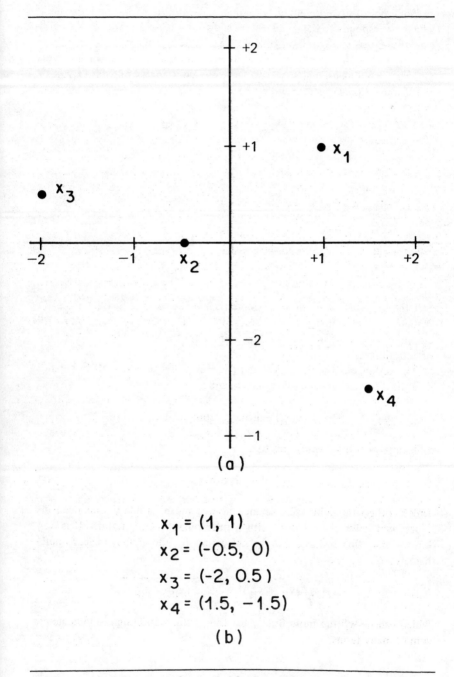

(a)

$x_1 = (1, 1)$
$x_2 = (-0.5, 0)$
$x_3 = (-2, 0.5)$
$x_4 = (1.5, -1.5)$

(b)

Figure 4: Relationship between Geometrical Configuration and Numerical Coordinates

$$d_{ij} = \sqrt{\sum_{r=1}^{R} (x_{ir} - x_{jr})^2}$$

It is natural to arrange the distances d_{ij} into a matrix like that for the data values: when $I = 4$ this is

$$\begin{bmatrix} d_{11} & d_{12} & d_{13} & d_{14} \\ d_{21} & d_{22} & d_{23} & d_{24} \\ d_{31} & d_{32} & d_{33} & d_{34} \\ d_{41} & d_{42} & d_{43} & d_{44} \end{bmatrix}$$

It can easily be verified that:

$$d_{ii} = 0 \quad \text{for all i,}$$
$$d_{ij} = d_{ji} \quad \text{for all i and j (symmetry).}$$

Thus the main diagonal of the matrix (from upper left to lower right) consists of 0's, and the matrix is symmetric. Distances also have other important properties which we will not go into here.

DIFFERENT TYPES OF MDS

The central motivating concept of multidimensional scaling is that the *distances* d_{ij} *between the points should correspond to the proximities* δ_{ij}. A good way to see the correspondence between the d_{ij} and the δ_{ij} is by a *scatter diagram* (or Shepard diagram) like those in Figures 5A and 5B. In each diagram, each point corresponds to one pair (i, j), and has coordinates (δ_{ij}, d_{ij}). Thus the horizontal axis displays the proximities and the vertical axis displays the distances. (Such diagrams are sometimes displayed with the axes interchanged, as in Figure 5C.)

Suppose the proximities are *dis*similarities, as in Figure 5A. We want small dissimilarities to correspond to small distances, and large dissimilarities to large distances. Geometrically, this means that the points in the scatter diagram should form a rising pattern, low on the left (small dissimilarity—small distance points) and high on the right (large dissimilarity—large distance points). Figure 5A fits this requirement extremely well: such a clean-cut relationship is extremely unusual in practice. On the other hand, if the proximities are similarities, as in Figure 5C, we want the points to form a falling pattern. Figure 5C does indeed fit this description, though the relationship has a rather large amount of scatter in it.

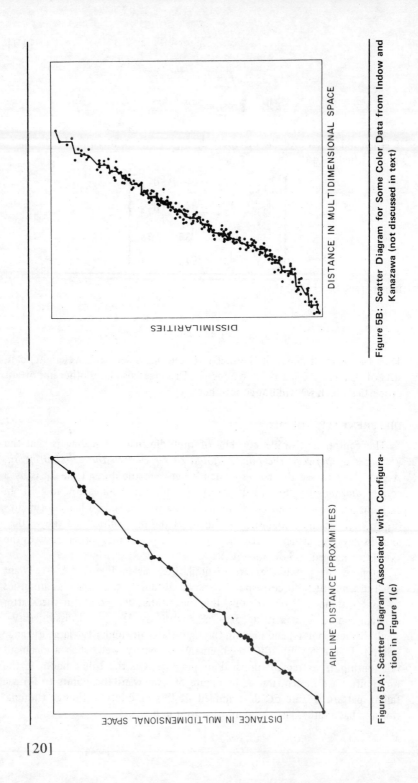

DISTANCE IN MULTIDIMENSIONAL SPACE

DISSIMILARITIES

Figure 5B: Scatter Diagram for Some Color Data from Indow and Kanazawa (not discussed in text)

AIRLINE DISTANCE (PROXIMITIES)

DISTANCE IN MULTIDIMENSIONAL SPACE

Figure 5A: Scatter Diagram Associated with Configuration in Figure 1(c)

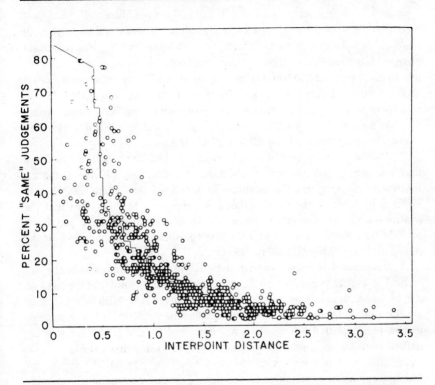

Figure 5C: Scatter Diagram Associated with Morse Code Configuration in Figure 3

The traditional way to describe a desired pattern or relationship is by means of a *formula*, such as $d = 3 + 10\delta$, or $d = 5 + 2\sqrt{\delta}$. However, it is seldom possible in advance to know the numerical values of the coefficients in the formula, so the pattern is usually described by a formula which has some unknown coefficients in it, for example,

$$d = a + b\delta,$$

where the values of a and b for a given set of data must be discovered along with everything else during the numerical calculation. This particular formula describes a straight-line relationship between δ and d. Another significant type of relationship is,

$$d = b\delta,$$

which describes a straight-line relationship where the straight line goes through the origin of the graph.

Any given formula d = f(δ) like those above corresponds to a particular type of relationship between δ and d. We can adjust the numerical calculation procedure to aim for any type of relationship we wish, and each type of relationship corresponds to a different type of MDS. There is one important proviso, however. It is seldom possible in practice to achieve the desired relationship perfectly. As in Figure 5C, there is often a substantial scatter about the desired curve or straight line. Even Figure 5A, where the relationship looks so clean, if we adjusted the calculation to aim for the relationship d = bδ, we could not achieve this perfectly. (To indicate this imperfection, the sign $\cong$ for *approximate* equality is often used.)

Furthermore, many sets of data "have a mind of their own" in the sense that the configuration which is obtained, and consequently the distances, the scatter diagram, and the relationship between δ and d, are only slightly affected by what relationship is aimed for. However, to the extent that the relationship aimed for differs from the intrinsic relationship, a penalty is paid. In part this consists of an alteration (presumably a degradation) of the configuration. Usually this alteration is mild.

A relationship d = f(δ) described by an ordinary formula uses the numerical or metric properties of the proximities. For example, in the formula d = bδ, if we double δ, we also double d. For this reason, MDS based on aiming for a relationship like one of these is called *metric* MDS. It is also possible to aim for a relationship which is not described by any formula, but is described *only* by the fact that we want d = f(δ) to describe a *rising* pattern. Geometrically, this means a curve (or a series of points) like Figure 5A which keeps rising as we move to the right. For this purpose, any increasing curve is as good as any other, whether it is straight, has one bend in it, two bends like a sigmoid curve, or 10 bends. Whether or not a curve (or a series of points) is rising does not depend on the numerical metric properties of the proximities. It does not depend on sums, products, or differences of the proximities. It only depends on the *rank order* or the proximities. For this reason, the name *nonmetric* MDS is used to describe MDS in which an increasing function, or alternatively a decreasing function, is aimed for.

The first metric procedure for MDS, due to Richardson (1938), aims for d = bδ. It is based on a theorem by Young and Householder (1938), which gives a method for constructing the configuration from the given (Euclidean) distances among the points, by a method closely related to factor analysis. Torgerson (1958) rediscovered this method and extended it to aim for the relationship d = a + bδ, by a two-stage procedure: first, and "additive constant" is determined and added to the raw proximities; second, the Young-Householder construction is performed. (Of historical interest are Boyden, 1933, and several later papers, which give a biological application of MDS, though not so named, of course. The proximity between species i and j was the strength of the reaction between serum i and an antiserum to j, and an ad hoc geometrical construction method was used.)

Hays, as described in Coombs (1964:444), suggested the first procedure for nonmetric MDS. His method was nonmetric in two senses: (1) the strong metric assumption of the Torgerson procedure was replaced by an assumption of an ordinal relationship between the proximities and the distances; and (2) only the rank order of stimuli on each dimension is determined.

Shepard (1962) focused attention on the relationship between proximities and distances, demonstrated that it was possible to derive metric MDS solutions assuming only an ordinal relationship between proximities and distances, and provided the first computer program to accomplish multidimensional scaling, which is nonmetric in this sense. Kruskal (1964a,b) built directly on Shepard's "analysis of proximities," but improved it in important ways; these advances were incorporated in the computer program M-D-SCAL and subsequently in KYST. As we shall explain in the next section, a numerical measure of goodness-of-fit was made central, and a systematic method for optimizing it was used to arrive at the configuration that provides the best fit to the data. Although the computer program allows for metric (linear, polynomial, etc.) as well as nonmetric functions, it is often mistakenly referred to as a procedure exclusively for nonmetric MDS. Although the original paper introducing the method was entitled, "Nonmetric Multidimensional Scaling," we feel the metric uses are quite as important as the nonmetric.

DEFINING AN OBJECTIVE FUNCTION

At this point, it is appropriate to say something about the computational procedure used to obtain the configuration from the data.* As we indicated before, there are many different computational approaches to MDS. Some of these clearly separate the *definition* of the desired configuration from the *computational procedure* used to obtain it. Other approaches make this separation less clear. In the most extreme cases, a computational procedure is described and the desired configuration is whatever is provided by the procedure.

We believe that a clear separation of definition and computational procedure has several important advantages, and historically there has been a strong trend in this direction. For this reason, we wish to describe a commonly used approach which makes this separation very clear. Furthermore, it provides a uniform approach to the different types of MDS described above. This method requires that we first define the desired solution before discussing the computational procedure.

---

*This section is more mathematical, and may be omitted.

We start by defining an *objective function*. (The same general concept is used in many fields under many names, such as criterion function, error function, evaluation function, merit function, goodness-of-fit function, badness-of-fit function, and so forth). For any given set of data and for any given configuration, the objective function yields a single number which shows how well (or how poorly) the data fit the configuration—i.e., it indicates how well the configuration represents the data.

The basic concept takes the form that:

$$f(\delta_{ij}) = d_{ij},$$

where f is of some specified type. One natural objective function can be formed as follows: suppose we have some function, f, of the specified type. (How we pick f is described below.) The discrepancy between $f(\delta_{ij})$ and d_{ij} is then:

$$f(\delta_{ij}) - d_{ij}.$$

These discrepancies are shown in Figure 6 as vertical line segments for a function f which is increasing. We measure the size of this discrepany by taking its square, since positive and negative discrepancies are equally undesirable. Then we take the sum of these squared discrepancies for all proximities, which yields the formula

$$\sum_i \sum_j [f(\delta_{ij}) - d_{ij}]^2.$$

Next, we divide by a scale factor in order to measure the squared discrepancies relative to a sensible measuring stick. The scale factor most commonly used is

$$\sum_i \sum_j d_{ij}^2.$$

Finally, for minor reasons which we will not go into here, we take the square root of the result. Thus, we obtain an objective function which we shall call "f-stress." The formula for f-stress is

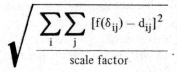

$$\sqrt{\frac{\sum_i \sum_j [f(\delta_{ij}) - d_{ij}]^2}{\text{scale factor}}}.$$

The larger f-stress is, the worse the configuration X and the function f jointly fit the data. Clearly we always have f-stress $\geqslant 0$, since the differences are

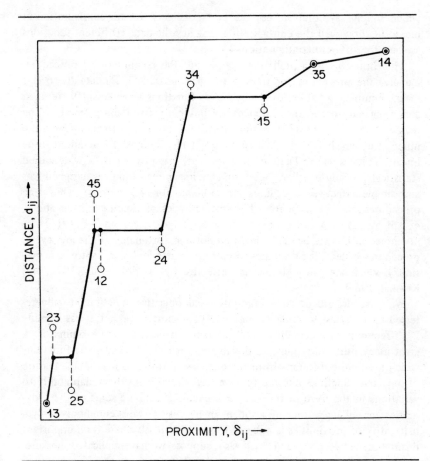

Figure 6: Illustration of the Discrepancies $\hat{d}_{ij} - d_{ij}$ that Enter into the Formula for Stress

squared. Furthermore, if f-stress = 0, then we have exact equality, that is, $f(\delta_{ij}) = d_{ij}$, for every proximity value, δ_{ij}. In this case, the representation is "perfect" in the special sense that δ_{ij} is perfectly related to d_{ij} by the function of the desired type. Of course, it is not possible to achieve an f-stress of 0 for most sets of data.

We want a measure of how well the configuration itself fits the data without the "f" entering in. We define our measure to be

$$\text{stress} (\Delta, X) = \min_{\text{all } f} \text{f-stress} (\Delta, X, f)$$

which simply says that we use the best possible f for this configuration in measuring how well the configuration matches the data. (Different functions are best for different configurations.)

This brings us to a preliminary aspect of the computational procedure, namely, the procedure for finding the best possible f. Finding the best f means minimizing f-stress over all possible functions when Δ and X are fixed and given, and hence the distances are indirectly fixed and given also. The denominator of the f-stress is then fixed, so this comes to minimizing the numerator, which is a residual sum of squares. Suppose f is required to be linear, $f(\delta) = a + b\delta$. Then finding the best f is just what the widely-used statistical procedure called "least squares linear regression" is designed for, and simple effective procedures are available for this purpose. The same procedures may be used for all the other types of functions listed above, except for $f(\delta) = \delta$ and f monotonic (increasing or decreasing). For $f(\delta) = \delta$, no choice of f has to be made. For f monotonic, fortunately, there are several procedures called "least squares monotonic regression" (or "isotonic regression") which are fairly simple and effective (see Barlow et al., 1972, and Kruskal, 1964b).

We have described one commonly used objective function, usually referred to as "stress formula 1," or stress 1 for short. A variant, stress formula 2, differs only in that a different scale factor is used as the denominator. A great many other variations are possible and reasonable, and some functions which look quite different from these are also possible. One desirable feature of objective functions like the two we have described is their adaptability to variations in the form of the data. For example, suppose some of the proximities are missing, either by accident or by design. (Most commonly, only a halfmatrix of proximities is collected, since frequently there is no important distinction between δ_{ij} and δ_{ji}.) Also, suppose we have replicated measurements, i.e., some or all of the proximities have been measured more than once. To adapt stress to these situations, all we need do is to sum the squared discrepancies over those proximities which we have, and omit from the sum those which are missing. (The same modification is made in the scale factor.) Another form of adaptability becomes apparent if we wish to reflect a different level of measurement error for different proximities: it is very easy to incorporate weights into the stress function for this purpose, and some programs allow for this.

Our general attitude is that the choice of an objective function is one of those arbitrary choices which must be made in any scientific endeavor. Practical experience suggests that the choice is not too critical, however, that is, the MDS results are unlikely to differ very much. Our choice can be supported by many parallels in statistics and other fields as well as by intuitive reasoning. However, the ultimate justification is that MDS "works" and is useful. Alternative objective functions are in use in the field of MDS, and there has been research directed to comparing their properties and usefulness. However, the choice among reasonable alternatives is not important to the average user, and the subject is outside the scope of this paper.

Now that we have an objective function, we can describe how it can be used to *define* a configuration X starting from the data Δ. The definition is quite simple, though finding the configuration is difficult. The idea is simply to pick the "best" configuration;[1] that is, the configuration which yields the best possible value of the objective function, which we will refer to as $\hat{X}$ (read X-hat). In other words, given Δ, we want to find $\hat{X}$ which produces the smallest possible value for stress (Δ, X). In symbols we define the desired configuration or solution to be the configuration $\hat{X}$ for which

$$\text{stress } (\Delta, \dot{X}) = \min_{\text{all } X} \text{ stress } (\Delta, X).$$

COMPUTATIONAL PROCEDURE

One widely used procedure for *finding* the best configuration is the method of steepest descent. A full description is complex, and would require too much space for this paper, so we content ourselves with an analogy. (Recent textbooks on numerical analysis may be consulted for further information, though texts prior to 1965 seldom have much which pertains to our situation.) Imagine some rolling terrain, with hills and valleys. Each point of the terrain corresponds to an entire configuration (*not* to a point *in* the configuration). Each point of the terrain can be described by three coordinates—the altitude, and the two location coordinates, North-South and East-West. The location coordinates are analogous to all the coordinates of all the points of the configuration. (Of course, a configuration with I points in R-dimensional space has IR coordinates, and IR is far greater than two, so the analogy does not convey the full richness and difficulty of the situation.) The altitude is analogous to the objective function, that is, the altitude is the stress.

Seeking the configuration with minimum stress corresponds to seeking the point with minimum altitude, the lowest point of the terrain. However, since it is impossible to get any overview of the stress function, this is like seeking the lowest point of the terrain while blindfolded. We need a starting point for the search. Sometimes we pick any point in the terrain at random for this purpose: this is something like dropping a blindfolded parachutist on a dark night from a high-flying airplane onto the terrain (a rough analogy!). Next we proceed downhill from the starting point by steps. Imagine the same blindfolded parachutist, looking for the lowest point of the terrain. She stands on one foot, feels all around her with the other, picks out the direction which is most strongly downhill, and takes one step in that direction. She then repeats the procedure at the next location, and so on. Eventually she gets to a spot where no direction is downhill, and stops.

If the terrain does not have ripples and irregularities, then this spot is probably the lowest point of the valley she happened to get into. If the whole terrain is shaped like one vast bowl, so there is only one valley, the parachutist will be at the lowest point. If the terrain has only one central valley but has several slight irregularities, then there is a good chance she has reached the lowest point, but there is some chance she got trapped in the bottom of an irregularity. Any place where the parachutist can stop is called a "local minimum." If it is the lowest point of the terrain, it is called the global minimum. (In technically correct language, the global minimum is also a local minimum, but the phrase local minimum is frequently used to indicate a local minimum other than the global minimum.)

In practice, the possibility of finding a local minimum other than the global minimum is real. Fortunately, it will generally differ only slightly from the global minimum, for example, by the rearrangement of two or three nearby points within their own neighborhood. However, a local minimum *can* differ drastically from the global minimum. In such cases the configuration may not be interpretable. Also, its stress is usually much larger than the stress of the global minimum. Direct consideration of the stress value, and comparison of the stress with that of the next higher-dimensional and lower-dimensional solutions, may well suggest that a bad local minimum has been encountered. Whenever suspicion exists, investigation is possible by obtaining several different solutions using different starting configurations. (In terms of the analogy, the starting configuration is the place where the parachutist first lands on the ground. Using several different starting configurations is like dropping several parachutists at different spots, and letting them find their way downhill separately.) It is unlikely that the calculations would all converge to a common local minimum which is not the global minimum. Finally, when there is a local minimum very different from the global minimum but with stress almost as small, experience suggests that both stress values will be large, and that neither of the solutions will be of any use.

LOOKING AT THE SCATTER DIAGRAM

The scatter diagram for any configuration shows distances versus proximities, and the function f of specified type which best fits them. The diagram contains one point (δ_{ij}, d_{ij}) for each proximity. Once the best configuration has been found, the associated scatter diagram often contains useful information. Such diagrams are included in this paper.

The values $f(\delta_{ij})$ are often called the "fitted distances" and denoted by $\hat{d}_{ij}$ (read "d-hat-i-j"; they are also sometimes called "disparities"). However, it is important to remember that the fitted distances are *not* distances, but simply numbers which are fitted *to* the distances.

In examining a scatter diagram, the first thing to look for is to see how well the scatter of points fit the function f. Of course, the stress is a numerical measure of the badness-of-fit, but a direct visual impression is useful in addition to the numerical value. Suppose the horizontal axis is at the d = 0 level, as usual. Then stress 1 has a geometrical interpretation:

$$\frac{\text{root mean square vertical discrepancy between point and curve}}{\text{root mean square distance from point to axis}}.$$

Suppose we draw a horizontal line at the level d = d̄. Then stress 2 has the geometrical interpretation

$$\frac{\text{root mean square vertical discrepancy between point and curve}}{\text{root mean square distance from point to line}}.$$

MDS is very robust in the sense that the configuration obtained using one assumption about f is not very different from that using another assumption. (When the number I of objects is small, however, this robustness may disappear.) As a result, whatever assumption we make about f, the scatter diagram may clearly show us that the data demand or suggest some other type of function. The way this shows up is by the clear formation of the points around some curve (not drawn in) other than f. For example, if we assumed f linear instead of merely increasing for the data used in Figure 5B, we would get virtually the same configuration, and hence a scatter diagram with the points located almost the same as the one shown, together with a straight line function for f that is the best straight line approximation to this clearly indicated curve. If the points clearly show some other curve than the one plotted, then the value of stress will be unduly inflated by the inappropriate assumption made about f. It is best to reanalyze the data using a more appropriate assumption.

When we assume f to be montonic, the curves almost always have a characteristic jagged appearance (as in figures 5A, 5B, 5C, and 6). The individual zigs and zags seldom have any real meaning, in the sense that quite different zigs and zags would appear if we collected new data. However, the general shape of a smooth curve drawn through the points on the scatter diagram is often meaningful. For example, the bend in the lower left of Figure 5B probably reflects an end effect induced by the particular data collection method.

Another important phenomenon called *degeneracy* shows up very clearly on the scatter diagram. This phenomenon means that the points of the configuration are strongly clumped—most of the points are on or close to a very small number of locations. This phenomenon can occur primarily under the following conditions: (1) nonmetric scaling is being used; (2) the objects have a natural clustering, usually of three or less clusters, and the dissimilarities *between* objects in different clusters are all (or almost all) larger than the dissimilarities *within* each cluster. Under these circumstances, all or almost all the points for the objects in a single cluster will converge to a single location. Furthermore, the stress will converge toward 0, though it may not reach 0 in practice. If there are three or four clusters, the corresponding locations will frequently form an equilateral triangle or tetrahedron. If degeneracy occurs, the clustering it springs from should be noted and considered, but no other conclusions should be drawn. In particular, the very small stress should not be taken as indicating good fit in a substantive sense, since it is obtained by violating two tacit assumptions: that the true relationship between distance and proximity is smooth, and that points should only lie in the same position if the corresponding objects function as virtually identical. Metric analysis, or reanalysis of each cluster separately, is desirable in these instances.

The scatter diagram for a degenerate solution has a characteristic appearance like a staircase consisting of a few very large steps. A great many of the points are on or very near a few horizontal segments. This appearance results from the fact that almost all the d_{ij} take on a small number of distinct values. (One of these values is always 0, and it occurs for all distances within each cluster.)

2. INTERPRETATION OF THE CONFIGURATION

APPLICATION TO PERCEPTIONS OF NATIONS

Having discussed many of the basic concepts of MDS, we are now ready to work through an application to real data. The data are from a pilot study on perceptions of nations conducted in March 1968 (Wish, 1971; Wish, Deutsch, and Biener, 1970). Each of the 18 students (in a psychological measurement course taught by Wish) participating in the study rated the degree of overall similarity between twelve nations on a scale ranging from 1 for "very different" to 9 for "very similar." There were no instructions concerning the characteristics on which these similarity judgments were to be made; this was information to discover rather than to impose.

The first step of the data analysis was to compute the mean similarity rating for each of the 66 pairs (all combinations of the 12 nations). As illustrated in Figure 7, these mean ratings were arranged in matrix form to be acceptable as input to an MDS analysis. Thus, Russia and Yugoslavia were perceived to be more similar to each other (mean = 6.67) than any other pair of nations, while China-Brazil and USA-Congo were judged to be the most dissimilar pairs (mean = 2.39).

	BRZ	CON	CUB	EGY	FRA	IND	ISR	JPN	CHI	RUS	USA	YUG
BRAZIL	—											
CONGO	4.83	—										
CUBA	5.28	4.56	—									
EGYPT	3.44	5.00	5.17	—								
FRANCE	4.72	4.00	4.11	4.78	—							
INDIA	4.50	4.83	4.00	5.83	3.44	—						
ISRAEL	3.83	3.33	3.61	4.67	4.00	4.11	—					
JAPAN	3.50	3.39	2.94	3.83	4.22	4.50	4.83	—				
CHINA (MAINLAND)	2.39	4.00	5.50	4.39	3.67	4.11	3.00	4.17	—			
RUSSIA	3.06	3.39	5.44	4.39	5.06	4.50	4.17	4.61	5.72	—		
U.S.A.	5.39	2.39	3.17	3.33	5.94	4.28	5.94	6.06	2.56	5.00	—	
YUGOSLAVIA	3.17	3.50	5.11	4.28	4.72	4.00	4.44	4.28	5.06	6.67	3.56	—

Figure 7: Matrix of Mean Similarity Ratings for Twelve Nations

Rather than going into detail at this point regarding the choice of dimensionality, we shall simply start with the results obtained from a two-dimensional analysis of these data (using the KYST program).

The computer output included the list of coordinates for nations given in Figure 8A, and the plot of these values shown in Figure 8B.[2] The most common way of interpreting such a multidimensional solution is to look for lines in the space, possibly at right angles to each other, such that the stimuli projecting at opposite extremes of a line differ from each other in some easily describable way. This interpretive process is illustrated in Figure 8C by the two dashed lines superimposed on the preceding diagram (Figure 8B). Observe that the pro-Communist nations are at one end of Dim. 1′ (the line going from the lower left to the upper right), while the pro-Western nations are at the other end. Likewise, Dim. 2′ roughly distinguishes the economically (or technologically) developed nations from those that are less developed (the underdeveloped or "developing" nations). It seems reasonable, therefore, to interpret these dimensions as "Political Alignment" and "Economic Development," respectively.

Let us look now at how well distances in the two-dimensional configuration reflect the proximities data from which the space was derived. The computer output indicated that the stress (formula 1) of this configuration was .19. Although this was a sharp drop from the value of .39 obtained for a one-dimensional solution, it still indicates that the fit is far from perfect.

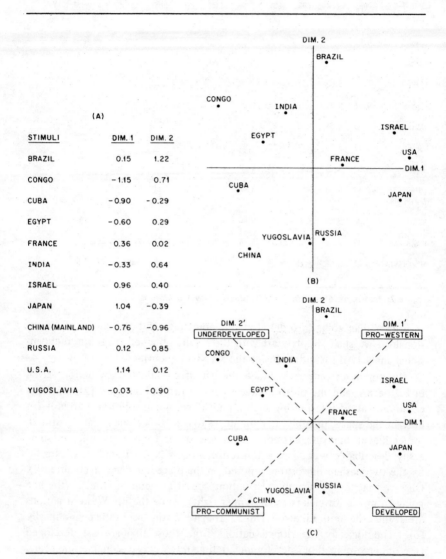

(A)

STIMULI	DIM. 1	DIM. 2
BRAZIL	0.15	1.22
CONGO	−1.15	0.71
CUBA	−0.90	−0.29
EGYPT	−0.60	0.29
FRANCE	0.36	0.02
INDIA	−0.33	0.64
ISRAEL	0.96	0.40
JAPAN	1.04	−0.39
CHINA (MAINLAND)	−0.76	−0.96
RUSSIA	0.12	−0.85
U.S.A.	1.14	0.12
YUGOSLAVIA	−0.03	−0.90

Figure 8: Stimulus Coordinates from a Two-Dimensional KYST Analysis of the Nation Similarities Data (Fig. 7) are Listed in (A) and Plotted in (B). The Dashed Lines in (C) were Drawn on the MDS Configuration to Indicate the Subjective Interpretations of the Dimensions.

Given the small number of subjects, however, it is unclear whether the .19 stress value reflects unreliability or the existence of additional structure in the data matrix.

A simple way to answer this question is to examine the residuals associated with fitting a two-dimensional configuration. The residual for stimulus pair (i, j) is $d_{ij} - \hat{d}_{ij}$, that is, the difference between interpoint distance d_{ij} in the multidimensional space and the fitted distance $\hat{d}_{ij} = f(\delta_{ij})$. (These values are printed out by the KYST and M-D-SCAL programs when the option, "PRINT DISTANCES," is selected.)

Figure 9 shows the residuals, in matrix form, for this MDS solution. Inspection of the residuals shows that the two-dimensional space (Figure 8) overestimates (relative to the similarities data in Figure 7) distances between nations that are geographically close, and underestimates distances between nations that are far apart geographically or culturally. For example, according to the similarities data, Cuba should be closer to Brazil in the space (residual = +.78) and China should be closer to Japan (residual = +.52). On the other hand, France should be further away in the space from India and Israel (residuals = −.66 and −.64, respectively).

The systematic pattern of residuals provides an indication that two dimensions do not represent all the structure in the proximity matrix. In this regard, stress goes down to .11 in three dimensions and to .05 in four. If a larger

	BRZ	CON	CUB	EGY	FRA	IND	ISR	JPN	CHI	RUS	USA	YUG
BRAZIL	—											
CONGO	.28	—										
CUBA	.78	-.09	—									
EGYPT	-.04	-.36	-.40	—								
FRANCE	.10	.14	-.07	-.13	—							
INDIA	-.37	-.22	-.27	-.18	-.66	—						
ISRAEL	-.37	.05	.40	.45	-.64	-.05	—					
JAPAN	.25	.36	-.15	.18	-.57	.35	-.25	—				
CHINA (MAINLAND)	.00	.20	-.10	-.10	-.11	.30	.11	.52	—			
RUSSIA	-.02	.00	.12	-.01	-.15	.20	.15	-.10	.10	—		
U.S.A.	.43	.00	-.01	-.34	.17	.20	-.09	.09	.00	.35	—	
YUGOSLAVIA	.03	.38	.12	-.04	-.13	.05	.28	-.18	-.32	.00	-.04	—

Figure 9: Residuals from Two-Dimensional KYST Analysis of Similarities among Twelve Nations

number of nations had been included in this study, it would have been reasonable to conclude that a four-dimensional representation was most appropriate. However, with only I = 12 stimuli, it is unlikely that more than R = 2 or perhaps 3 stable dimensions can be determined. A rough rule of thumb is that there should be at least twice as many stimulus pairs as parameters to be estimated, to assure an adequate degree of statistical stability. When using a half matrix without diagonal, this means I(I−1)/2 ⩾ 2IR, or equivalently, that the number of stimuli minus one should be at least four times as great as the dimensionality (I−1 ⩾ 4R; empirical support for this rule of thumb exists mostly for R ⩽ 3). Interpretations of more dimensions than specified by this guideline should be regarded as very tentative until replicated in studies involving more stimuli (see Wish, Deutsch, and Biener, 1970).[3]

The multidimensional results from this study are likely to show only partial agreement with one's intuitions and with more objective information about economic development and political alignment. There are several reasons for this:

(1) the data reflect perceptions in 1968, and the world has changed a great deal since then,

(2) the subjects were not sophisticated about world politics and economics,

(3) one's intuitions may not perfectly match those of the subjects,

(4) the number of subjects was quite small,

(5) the data was forced to fit in two dimensions,

(6) the choice of axes was based on the experimenter's intuitions.

The choice of axis orientation can be handled objectively by use of multiple regression analysis. Moreover, the use of regression techniques enables the investigator to assess the validity of dimensional interpretations for the subject sample involved. In the next section we explain and illustrate the use of multiple regression for interpreting dimensions, and also point out other approaches for interpreting MDS results.

This example illustrates an important point about the interpretation of the MDS configuration. The coordinates printed out and plotted by the computer are not generally susceptible to direct interpretation. To understand why this is so, recall that they represent the positions of the points along the coordinate axes, that is, the projections of points on the axes. *Now it is permissible to rotate the configuration, and if we do so these projections change quite drastically.* The reason rotation is permissible is that the configuration is based on the distances between the points. These distances do not change when the configuration is rotated, so they contain no information whatsoever as to what rotational position is "correct" for the configuration. In fact, in typical MDS applications there is no such thing as a correct rotational position for the configuration, although certain positions may be more pleasing aesthetically, or more useful for some purposes. For that matter, there is in truth no correct orientation of a geographical map. Even though we are strongly accustomed to seeing North pointing upward, this is merely a convention which is not correct in any absolute sense.

It is, therefore, important to remember that the solutions to ordinary multidimensional scaling (as opposed to "individual differences scaling" or "three-way MDS," discussed in Chapter 4)) are always subject to rotation. Since the configuration may be freely rotated, the coordinate axes have no special significance, and are no more meaningful than lines in any other direction. Thus, the coordinates as printed out are no more likely to be meaningful than the projections of the points on any arbitrary line.

LINEAR REGRESSION FOR DIMENSIONAL INTERPRETATION

We have seen that directions in the MDS configuration may have interesting interpretations. In other words, positions in the configuration may be systematically associated with some characteristics of the items which were scaled. Indeed, discovering which characteristics show up this way is one major reason for the use of MDS.

In useful or interesting applications, the characteristics we discover in this way are seldom totally unsuspected or surprising. On the other hand, they are usually part of a much longer list of characteristics which might just as plausibly have appeared. One useful role of MDS is to indicate which particular characteristics are important in contrast to others which are just as plausible.

One practical way to discover these characteristics is simply by looking at the configuration and recalling what is known about the objects. However, this method is limited in several ways. First, there is a difficulty which should not be important but often is, namely, forgetting that *all* directions should be examined, not only the directions of the coordinate axes. Second, if the configuration is in three or more dimensions, it is quite difficult to examine all directions visually. The only directions that are easy to examine are those lying within one of the planes chosen for visual display. These are normally only the coordinate planes, and sometimes not all of the coordinate planes are displayed. Other directions can be examined visually to some extent by making a vigorous mental effort, particularly if you have a good spatial imagination, but it is not easy or reliable. Third, when an apparent relationship is found between some direction in the configuration and some characteristic of the items, it is not always clear whether or not it is genuine. If the relationship is very strong, there will be no doubt, but if it is weaker, it is necessary to guard against the human tendency to find patterns whether or not they exist. This is one primary purpose of statistical coefficients and tests. While such procedures are quite practical for visually determined directions, when we want to carry out such tests it is usually better and more convenient to determine the direction and carry out the procedure in a unified way.

The method which is easiest to understand and most commonly used is based on linear regression. We state briefly the most important aspects of linear regression for our purpose. Suppose we have some variable associated with the items which we suspect may have a systematic relationship to position in the configuration. One way to see if it does is to perform a linear multiple regression using this variable as the dependent variable and the coordinates of the configuration as the independent variables. In the compact jargon of statistics, we can refer to this as regressing the variable over the coordinates of the configuration, or simply regressing the variable over the configuration. What this means is that we seek some weighted combination of the coordinates of the configuration which agrees with or "explains" the variable as well as possible. The multiple correlation coefficient is one measure of how well this can be done.

Suppose the configuration is three-dimensional, and the $i-$th item has coordinates (x_{i1}, x_{i2}, x_{i3}). Suppose the variable has value v_i for the $i-$th item. Then this means that we are looking for coefficients a, b_1, b_2, b_3 such that the function values

$$a + b_1 x_{i1} + b_2 x_{i2} + b_3 x_{i3}$$

agree with the values v_i as well as possible. By far the most common method, called least squares linear regression, is to choose the coefficients so as to minimize

$$\Sigma [v_i - (a + \sum_{r=1}^{3} b_r x_{ir})]^2$$

This is very widely used, and many different computer programs are available. Also, a great deal of theory and practical experience have been built up (see Appendix A for some explanation).

Perceived Relatedness Among Societal Problems

The use of linear multiple regression for interpreting dimensions can be clarified by an example. The data are from a pilot study dealing with perceived relatedness among various societal problems (for example, war, pollution, poverty, crime, and violence). The study was conducted in 1972 by M. Wish and J. D. Carroll, in collaboration with W. Kluver and J. Martin of Experiments in Art and Technology, Inc.

In the part of the study described here, 14 subjects rated the degree of relatedness between all pairwise combinations of 22 societal problems, and then rated the same stimuli singly on 15 bipolar scales.[4] For example, one of the rating scales ranged from 0 for "not responsibility of local government" to 9 for "strong responsibility of local government." The 22 x 22 matrix of average relatedness judgments was analyzed by MDS (using the KYST program), while the bipolar scale ratings guided the interpretation of dimensions.

A three-dimensional space seemed most appropriate for the relatedness data (stress = .41 in one dimension, .23 in two, .15 in three, .12 in four, .10 in five, and .08 in six dimensions). The stimulus coordinates on those dimensions are listed in the first three columns of Figure 10. The first step toward the interpretation of dimensions was to average subjects' ratings of every stimulus on each of the 15 bipolar scales. For example, the last four columns of Figure 10 show mean ratings of stimuli on some of the bipolar scales. The next step was to use a multiple regression procedure (Chang and Carroll's 1968 PROFIT program was used) to regress mean ratings of stimuli on each scale over the three dimensions listed in Figure 10.

The fourth column of Figure 11 indicates the multiple correlation between the three dimensions and the respective rating scales. For example, the multiple correlation is .841 for the third scale. Four of the multiple correlations are significant at the .001 level, and two others reach the .05 significance level.[5] There is no set of weights that can be applied to the three dimensions to get statistically significant correlations for any of the other rating scales.

The first three columns of Figure 11 show the optimum weights corresponding to each multiple correlation. (These are the direction cosines, that is, regression coefficients normalized so that their sum of squares equals 1.000 for every scale.) For example, when weights of $-.262$, $-.863$, and $-.432$ are given to dimensions 1, 2 and 3, respectively, the correlation between the resulting composite and mean ratings on the twelfth scale is .767.

In order for a rating scale (or any other variable) to provide a satisfactory interpretation of a dimension, two conditions are necessary: (1) the multiple correlation for the scale must be high (indicating that the scale can be well fitted by the coordinates of the configuration), and (2) the scale must have a high regression weight on that dimension (indicating that the angle between the dimension and the direction of the associated scale is small). Although it is desirable to have multiple correlations in the .90's for a good interpretation

STIMULI	DIM 1	DIM 2	DIM 3	(3) AFFECTS ME	(4) AFFECTS MOST PEOPLE	(10) TECHNO-LOGICAL PROBLEM	(12) LOCAL RESPONSI-BILITY
A. CONSUMER EXPLOITATION	0.78	-0.31	0.71	5.71	8.07	2.54	6.92
B. CRIME AND VIOLENCE	-0.67	0.15	0.24	3.50	6.07	2.77	8.46
C. DETERIORATION OF PUBLIC EDUCATION	0.15	-0.30	-0.91	3.00	6.50	5.62	8.08
D. DRUG AND ALCOHOL ABUSE	-1.03	0.59	-0.29	2.43	5.29	3.23	7.54
E. FAILURES IN WELFARE	0.86	-0.52	-0.59	2.29	4.71	2.46	7.77
F. IMBALANCES IN POLITICAL REPRESENTATION	-0.16	-1.03	0.12	4.50	5.57	2.77	7.85
G. INADEQUATE HEALTH CARE	-0.26	0.49	-0.90	2.57	6.29	5.00	7.62
H. INEFFECTIVENESS OF LOCAL GOVERNMENT	0.25	-0.83	-0.40	4.43	6.07	2.62	8.15
I. INEQUITIES IN THE JUDICIAL SYSTEM	-0.37	-0.71	0.91	2.64	5.57	2.00	8.08
J. INFLATION	0.16	0.92	0.66	4.64	7.57	2.62	4.38
K. JOB DISCRIMINATION	-0.97	-0.10	0.45	2.21	4.43	1.62	7.62
L. MISUSES OF TECHNOLOGY	0.98	0.52	-0.01	4.71	7.29	6.85	5.77
M. NEGLECT OF PUBLIC TRANSPORTATION	1.07	-0.83	-0.24	5.43	6.50	6.38	8.00
N. OVERPOPULATION	0.18	0.66	-0.78	5.79	7.79	5.03	5.54
O. POLLUTION OF THE ENVIRONMENT	1.23	0.16	-0.42	6.86	8.21	7.38	8.38
P. POVERTY	-0.32	0.26	-0.13	3.07	4.64	3.85	7.54
Q. PUBLIC AND PRIVATE GREED	0.49	-0.11	0.41	4.71	6.79	2.08	7.38
R. RACISM AND BIGOTRY	-0.64	-0.32	0.40	3.71	5.29	2.08	7.38
S. SUBSTANDARD HOUSING	-0.14	-0.00	0.04	2.43	4.29	6.15	7.54
T. UNEMPLOYMENT	-0.48	0.54	0.10	2.14	3.79	6.31	6.92
U. URBAN DECAY	0.03	0.04	-0.24	4.43	6.43	5.92	8.23
V. WAR	0.59	0.74	0.87	5.36	7.79	4.46	5.08

Figure 10: Three-Dimensional KYST Solution for Averaged Relatedness Ratings of 22 Societal Problems (shown in the first three columns) and Mean Ratings of These Stimuli on Four of the Bipolar Scales

POSITIVE POLES OF RATING SCALES	REGRESSION WEIGHTS (DIRECTION COSINES)			MULT. CORR.
	DIM. 1	DIM. 2	DIM. 3	
1. VERY IMPORTANT	0.538	0.765	-0.354	0.491
2. VERY INTERESTED	0.909	0.386	0.160	0.364
3. AFFECTS ME A GREAT DEAL	0.994	0.045	0.105	0.841**
4. AFFECTS MOST PEOPLE	0.938	0.342	0.049	0.804**
5. ACTION URGENTLY NEEDED	0.557	0.424	-0.714	0.301
6. ECONOMIC PROBLEM	0.329	0.942	-0.072	0.523
7. MORAL PROBLEM	-0.170	-0.117	0.979	0.519
8. POLITICAL PROBLEM	0.364	-0.685	-0.631	0.300
9. ORGANIZATIONAL PROBLEM	0.320	-0.474	-0.820	0.638*
10. TECHNOLOGICAL PROBLEM	0.612	0.416	-0.672	0.767**
11. RESPONSIBILITY OF FEDERAL GOVERNMENT	-0.032	0.736	0.677	0.437
12. RESPONSIBILITY OF LOCAL GOVERNMENT	-0.262	-0.863	-0.432	0.767**
13. RESPONSIBILITY OF NON-PROFIT INSTITUTIONS	0.592	0.435	-0.679	0.409
14. RESPONSIBILITY OF PROFIT-MAKING INSTITUTIONS	0.555	0.767	0.320	0.599*
15. RESPONSIBILITY OF PEOPLE DIRECTLY AFFECTED	0.302	-0.859	-0.414	0.386

** = $F_{3,18}$ SIGNIFICANT AT LESS THAN .001 LEVEL;

* = SIGNIFICANT AT LESS THAN .05.

Figure 11: Multiple Regression of Bipolar Scale Ratings on Dimensions of Relatedness among Societal Problems

of a dimension, correlations in the .80's and upper .70's have to suffice in many instances. Of course, the higher the value, the more confidence that can be placed in the interpretation of the particular dimension. As a minimal requirement, the multiple correlation should be statistically significant at the .01 level or better.

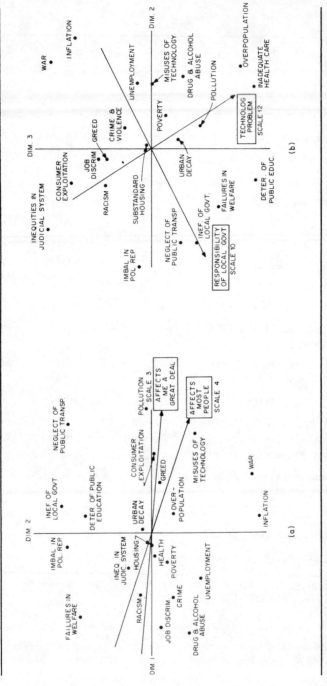

Figure 12: Three-Dimensional Configuration Obtained by the KYST Program for Perceived Relatedness among 22 Societal Problems. Dimensions 1 and 2 are Plotted in (a), while Dimensions 2 and 3 are Shown in (b). Vectors for the Rating Scales Defining the Dimensions were Determined by Linear Regression Analyses.

An interpretation can be given immediately to the first dimension, since the third scale has a relatively high multiple correlation (.841), and as shown in Figure 12A, the associated "property vector" almost coincides with that dimension. (A regression weight of .994 corresponds to an angle of 6 degrees since cosine($6°$) = .994.) The fourth scale also has a high weight on the first dimension. Accordingly, this dimension was interpreted as "large versus small effect on people."

Figure 12B shows the locations of the 22 societal problems on the plane defined by the second and third dimensions. Vectors are shown for the other two rating scales that have reasonable multiple correlations. Although these multiple R's are lower than desired, it seems reasonable to interpret the dimensions of this plane as "Technological versus Non-Technological Problem" and "Local versus Non-Local Government Responsibility." A more satisfying interpretation of these dimensions might be obtained by thinking of other variables that better distinguish stimuli at opposite extremes of various directions in this plane, and then including relevant scales in another study.

Perceived Association Among Psychological Traits

Another interesting example where multiple regression analysis clarified the interpretation of dimensions is a study by Rosenberg, Nelson, and Vivekananthan (1968) of perceived co-occurrences of psychological traits. The subjects' task was to sort trait terms (e.g., sociable, sincere) written on slips of paper into categories so that traits tending to go together in the same individual are put in the same pile. For the present purposes it suffices to discuss the two-dimensional solution obtained (using the M-D-SCAL program) from proximities among 60 traits. (The proximities were based on the frequencies of co-occurrence for pairs of traits.) As shown in Figure 13A, three properties, corresponding to the factors from the semantic differential were fit into the space by linear multiple regression (Osgood, Suci, and Tannenbaum, 1957): "Good versus Bad" (or "Evaluation"), "Hard versus Soft" (or "Potency"), and "Active versus Passive" (or "Activity"). These three variables were obtained as the median of ratings by many subjects of the extent to which each trait name indicated the particular property, for example, the extent to which "persistent" was a good versus bad trait.

The multiple correlation is high for good—bad (R = .878), moderate for hard—soft (R = .702), and low for active-passive (R = .427). Moreover, the directions for the first two of these properties are almost at right angles (83 degrees). Although "Good versus Bad" and "Hard versus Soft" provide a reasonable interpretation of the dimensions, Rosenberg et al. (1968) felt that an alternative interpretation was at least as appropriate. Notice that traits that are intellectually desirable (e.g., scientific, skillful, intelligent) are in the

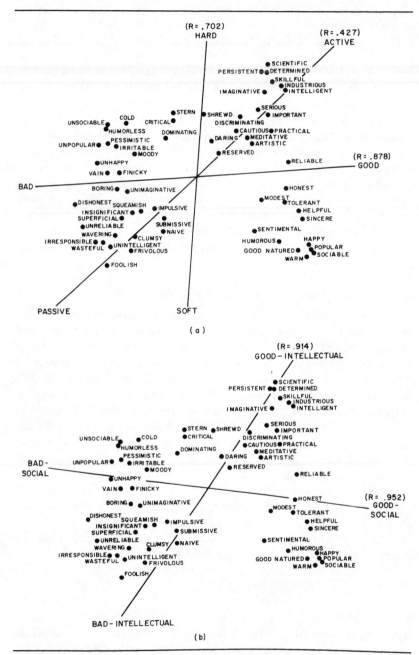

Figure 13: Two-Dimensional Space Obtained by Rosenberg et al. for Perceived Association among 60 Traits. Lines Drawn on the Configuration Show Directions of Best Fit for the Associated Property Vectors.

upper right corner, while those that are intellectually undesirable (e.g., foolish, frivolous, unintelligent) are in the lower left corner. Similarly, the socially desirable traits (e.g., warm, sociable, good natured) are in the lower right as contrasted with the socially undesirable traits in the upper left (unsociable, humorless, cold).

To test this alternative interpretation of social and intellectual desirability, the investigators got one group of subjects to rate each trait on a seven point scale "according to whether a person who exhibited each of the traits would be good or bad in his intellectual activities," and another group to rate each trait in relation to how good or bad it was for social activities.

Figure 13B shows that these two variables can be fit very well in the space—.914 for "Good-Intellectual versus Bad-Intellectual" and .952 for "Good-Social versus Bad-Social." These two directions are not perpendicular to each other; rather, the angle between them is 65 degrees. It should be pointed out that although perpendicular axes are simpler and hence scientifically preferable, nonperpendicular (oblique) axes may often provide a better characterization of the "real world" (see Harshman, 1970).

The fact that more than two properties can be fit into a two-dimensional space should not be regarded as alarming. Rather, the investigators were pleased with the possibility of alternative interpretations of their results. They proposed that an interpretation based on "hard" versus "soft" and "good" versus "bad" focuses on the connotative meaning of the traits, whereas the interpretation based on social and intellectual desirability is concerned more with denotative meaning.

Before leaving the topic of linear regression for dimensional interpretation, one potential problem should be pointed out. When the regressed variable is based on preference ratings, the use of mean ratings based on an entire group can be misleading. It is desirable to determine separate vectors of mean ratings for identifiable subgroups (e.g., Democrats, Republicans, Independents) in order to get meaningful regression weights (see Wish and Carroll, 1974).

NEIGHBORHOOD INTERPRETATION OF MDS CONFIGURATIONS

Dimensional interpretation is the most common approach used in MDS as well as in factor analysis. (Of course the word "factor" rather than "dimension" is used in factor analysis.) Through the use of multiple regression, a very simple, statistically supported description can be given of the major patterns in the data.

Sometimes, however, structure can be observed in the multidimensional space in addition to or instead of that provided by dimensional interpretation. For example, neighborhoods or regions of the space may have meaning

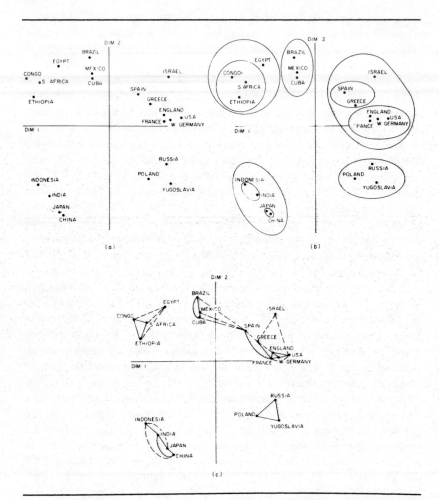

Figure 14: Two-Dimensional Configuration for Cultural Similarity among 21 Nations. The Loops Drawn on Configuration in (b) are Based on Hierarchical Clustering Analysis of these Data. Solid Lines between Stimuli in (c) Indicate Strong Proximity (as determined by the data), while the Dashed Lines Reflect Moderate Proximity Values.

associated with other shared characteristics. This often happens, for example, when a two-dimensional solution is obtained for data whose appropriate dimensionality is higher. An important reason why a neighborhood interpretation can reveal other patterns in the data is that its focus is primarily on the small distances (large similarities), while a dimensional approach attends most to the large distances.

Guttman (1965) has argued that a neighborhood or pattern approach is preferable to the traditional dimensional approach. In this regard, his smallest space analyses of correlations between mental tests have revealed important patterns in the data (such as simplexes, circumplexes, and radexes) missed in prior factor analyses. Used in conjunction with facet theory, Guttman has been successful in identifying the characteristics shared by stimuli in the same region of a multidimensional space.

Our point of view is somewhat more eclectic: use any means at your disposal to understand as much of the data and results as possible. Thus a neighborhood interpretation can be used to supplement and clarify the dimensions rather than to compete with them.

Figure 14A gives an example where a neighborhood interpretation seems more reasonable than a dimensional one. The proximities data were based on subjects' judgments about the cultural similarity of 21 nations. (The study as a whole is described in Wish, 1970, and in Wish and Carroll, 1974. However, this particular analysis has not previously been reported.)

If a dimensional interpretation were attempted, we might say that the horizontal axis separates European from non-European cultures, white from nonwhite, or perhaps Northern from Southern countries. By a stretch of the imagination one might even give an East versus West interpretation to the vertical dimension, since it contrasts the East Asian and Eastern European countries with the others. It seems less forced, however, to simply state that nations whose cultures are similar tend to cluster in the space. It is not strictly geographical since, for example, the United States and Mexico are rather far apart, and so are Israel and Egypt. The U.S. clusters with the Western European countries from which its culture is primarily derived, while Mexico is grouped with the Latin American countries. Note that the African countries are at the upper left, the East Asian countries are at the lower left, and the Eastern European countries are at the lower right of the space.

EMBEDDING OTHER INFORMATION IN
THE MDS CONFIGURATION

One way to locate or interpret neighborhoods involves the application of clustering techniques. Since this topic is discussed in another paper in this series, all we wish to say here is that there are systematic methods for finding clusters based directly on the proximity matrix. The clusters can be drawn in the multidimensional space as loops around the relevant stimulus points. Once this is done, we can seek some characteristic common to the objects in a cluster. Usually this is done subjectively, as an act of creative interpretation. Any labelling then gives meaning to the neighborhood where the cluster is located. We can predict that objects not previously studied, but having this characteristic would locate themselves in this neighborhood if more data were collected and analyzed. Figure 14B shows the clusters from a hierarchical clustering procedure (Johnson, 1967) drawn on the two-dimensional configuration for cultural similarity among nations. The fact that the loops are quite small shows there is a good correspondence between neighborhoods in the MDS configuration and clusters determined by hierarchical clustering analysis.

It is often desirable to supplement closeness in the configuration with closeness based directly on the proximities data, because neighborhoods in a low-dimensional (two or three-dimensional) space may misrepresent the data from which they were derived. This will happen, for example, if more dimensions are needed to describe the data. Thus, in the two-dimensional space for Rosenberg's trait sorting data (Figure 13), some almost contradictory traits—cautious and daring, submissive and impulsive, meditative and practical—are very close together: a three-dimensional analysis of these data pulled these trait terms apart. Another explanation is that MDS does a much better job in representing larger distances (the global structure) than in representing small distances (the local structure). In fact, Graef and Spence (1976) have shown that discarding only the smallest third or the middle third of the dissimilarities does not disturb the reconstruction of the multidimensional space, but discarding the most dissimilar third of the values in the matrix (the smallest similarities) causes a severe degradation.

One simple way to embed information from the original data matrix in the multidimensional space is to draw a line between every pair of objects whose proximity exceeds some threshold value, as in Figures 14C and 15. (We want the lines to be between nearby objects, so lines are drawn for small dissimilarities or large similarities.) Usually it is desirable to use more than one threshold, which can be indicated by solid, dashed, and dotted lines.

The presence of long and haphazardly crossing lines (based on the proximities data) indicates a discrepancy between closeness in the data and closeness in the space. If the configuration is two-dimensional, each long line identifies a large residual that should be taken into consideration when interpreting the configuration. When the lines are drawn on a plane from a higher-dimensional space, the disagreement between the data and the neighborhoods may be due to the other dimensions. Clusters in two-dimensional configuration are probably not valid unless they are consonant with the lines, that is, the points within a cluster should be well connected with each other, and poorly connected with those outside the cluster.

Figure 14C shows how such lines are drawn on the space for the same cultural similarity data. The solid lines show the pairs that the data indicate to be most similar (culturally), while the dashed lines show the next most similar pairs. Since all lines are between points that are close together in the

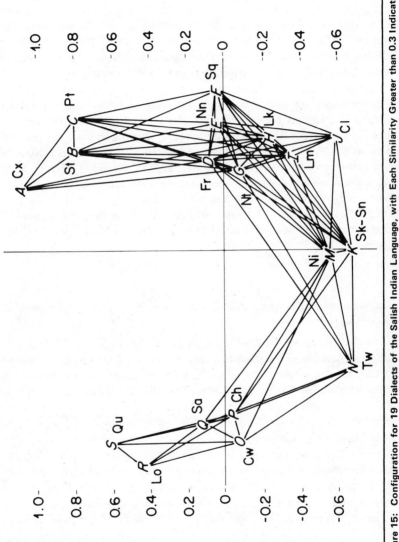

Figure 15: Configuration for 19 Dialects of the Salish Indian Language, with Each Similarity Greater than 0.3 Indicated by a Line. "Horseshoes" like this are not Uncommon (see p. 46 and Appendix B).

[47]

space, the spatial representation is quite compatible with the data. The lines do show other patterns of relationships more clearly, however; for example, the similarity of Spain to the Latin American countries on the one hand and to the Western European countries on the other. Observe, however, that there are no lines connecting the Latin American countries to the African countries despite the fact that these nations are close together in the configuration. This shows that the spatial distances do disagree somewhat with the proximities data (stress = .128).

As previously mentioned, the structure within neighborhoods sometimes provides a rather poor representation of the relative proximities between the stimuli involved. This is why we advocate drawing lines on the configuration to indicate closeness based on the original data. The internal structure of neighborhoods or clusters can also be clarified by doing separate MDS analyses for subsets of stimuli that are close to each other in the space. When enough stimuli are involved, such analyses may reveal dimensions that are obscured when all stimuli are analyzed simultaneously. Figure 15 illustrates a striking but not unusual phenomenon, which is discussed further in Appendix B.

3. DIMENSIONALITY

INTRODUCTION

The decision about the dimensionality to use for a given set of data is as much a substantive as a statistical question. Even if a good statistical method did exist for determining the "correct" or "true" dimensionality, this would not in itself suffice for assessing what dimensionality to use. Since MDS is almost always used as a descriptive model for representing and understanding the data, other considerations enter into decisions about the appropriate dimensionality, e.g., interpretability, ease of use, and stability.

In this chapter we are more concerned with the appropriate dimensionality (that which is most helpful in analyzing the data) than with the "correct" dimensionality (the hypothetical true dimensionality which underlies the data). It may be worthwhile to clarify the terminology, which is somewhat confusing. "Dimensionality" and the "number of dimensions" both refer to the number of coordinate axes, that is, the number of coordinate values used to locate a point in the space. This is basically the same notion as the number of factors in factor analysis. While "dimension" can also be used in the same sense, this may lead to ambiguity, since the word has several other meanings; for example, "dimension" can refer to a single coordinate axis, a direction of particular interest in a configuration, or some underlying characteristic of the objects under study.

Although a dimensional interpretation frequently involves one interpretation for each dimension of the space, the dimensionality is not necessarily the number of relevant characteristics involved. For example, in the Rosenberg et al. study (1968), there were four interpretable directions in the two-dimensional space of trait terms (Figure 13). Furthermore, although a characteristic or an attribute has an effect on the configuration, it may not contribute strongly enough to become visible as a separate dimension. This can be, for example, because the stimuli selected do not vary enough on that characteristic, because the characteristic is correlated with other dimensions, or because it is relevant to only a subset of the stimuli. Thus, although its presence may be demonstrable by other means, it will not necessarily show up as a dimension.

The number of interpretable directions or characteristics can also be less than the dimensionality of the space. For example, the investigator may only be able to interpret one or two of the dimensions even though the data seem to require a three-dimensional configuration. Furthermore, what is conceptually a single characteristic (such as "religious affiliation") may correspond to two (or conceivably more) dimensions when the characteristic is not describable as a single ordered variable.

"Dimension" also has several substantively different meanings: curvilinear dimensions may or may not be permitted; linearly dependent dimensions may or may not be permitted; and so on. Obviously, the dimensionality may be different for different meanings of dimension. Our primary concern in this section is how many dimensions to use in the configuration. We do not deal with dimensionality in its many other senses.

GOODNESS-OF-FIT

Some Precautions Before Choosing Dimensionality

Goodness-of-fit is a very important consideration in deciding how many dimensions are appropriate. A measure of fit (i.e., an objective function; see the discussion in Chapter 1) widely used in MDS is "stress," which is the square root of a normalized "residual sum of squares." Note that because larger values indicate worse fit, it would be more descriptive to call stress a badness-of-fit measure, a terminology which is sometimes used (Kruskal and Carroll, 1969).

This discussion will be phrased entirely in terms of stress. While this is convenient for us in view of our personal involvement with this measure, it is also the measure which has received the most systematic statistical study. Furthermore, although other measures have been proposed which might in principle be still better (notably by De Leeuw), there are fairly cogent arguments suggesting that this may be the best of the measures which have received wide use at this time.

When using stress or other values as a guide to dimensionality, it is assumed that each value is reasonably close to the true minimum stress value for the dimensionality involved, i.e., the smallest possible stress for that set of data in that dimensionality. Two reasons why this might not happen is that a merely local minimum value of stress might be obtained, as explained earlier, or that the convergence might be substantially incomplete (i.e., while the iterative procedure may be approaching the true minimum, it may not yet have gotten sufficiently close to the target). While there is no practical way to absolutely insure that a global minimum (or something very close to it) has been reached, there are precautions which help avoid incomplete convergence and local minima in most cases. We discuss these in the natural order of use.

(1) It is desirable, though by no means essential, to use a computer program (such as M-D-SCAL, TORSCA, or KYST) which systematically minimizes stress, or a program (such as ALSCAL) which minimizes some very similar quantity (such as SSTRESS). Remember that a given numerical value may indicate good fit for one measure and bad fit for another. For example, for the same degree of fit, stress values are much larger than ϕ-values (used by the SSA programs). Note also that values of stress 2 are generally more than double those of stress 1 for the same degree of fit.

(2) Each stress value results from an iterative computational procedure, i.e., a procedure in which the configuration is modified step by step to bring it into closer agreement with the data. If the procedure is substantially incomplete, then the stress value may be substantially larger than the true minimum for that dimensionality. It is essential to verify that this has not happened. In this regard, some computer programs (including KYST and M-D-SCAL) print out a phrase for each dimensionality indicating why the calculation terminated. A phrase such as "minimum was reached" indicates that under the interpretation rules built into the program, convergence appears to be complete. Because KYST and M-D-SCAL use conservative rules, this phrase may usually be relied on with these programs. On the other hand, a phrase such as "maximum number of iterations was reached" should always bring to mind the likelihood that convergence is substantially incomplete.

If the calculation terminated because the maximum number of iterations was reached, there is a substantial chance that convergence is incomplete. (If the program prints out a history of the calculation, an informed reading of this history often permits conclusions about how complete the convergence actually was.) If the calculation terminated because "the stress is sufficiently small" (and the limit used for this purpose, 0.01 in KYST and most versions of M-D-SCAL, is small enough), then it may be adequate for step (4) below and for choosing dimensionality to note that the true minimum stress is smaller than the limit value in this dimensionality, even though the true minimum is not known.

(3) Whenever a stress of 0 or sufficiently near to 0 (say .01 or less) is achieved, the possibility of a fully or partially degenerate solution should be investigated.

(4) It is also essential to examine the plot of stress versus dimensionality to see whether it has a normal appearance. Most important, stress should always decrease as dimensionality increases. Also, the points usually form a convex pattern, that is, the line connecting any two points on the plot is above the intermediate points. Violation of either of these conditions may suggest incomplete convergence or a local minimum. If reducing a single stress value would remove the violation, then we call that value suspiciously large, and suspicion attaches to the associated solution. This is quite important, because it is the only simple automatic clue which suggests a local minimum.

A suspiciously large stress may come about because of incomplete convergence. This is particularly common for the highest-dimensional solution in programs (such as KYST and M-D-SCAL), which first compute the highest-dimensional solution, then drop one coordinate to form the starting configuration for the next lower-dimensional solution. When the highest-dimensional stress is the only suspicious value, this possibility should immediately come to mind.

An apparently abnormal plot can occur when calculation for several solutions stopped due to "stress sufficiently small." In this case, there is no reason to expect stress to decrease with dimensionality *among* these solutions. (However, if a lower-dimensional solution has sufficiently small stress and a higher-dimensional solution does not get down to the same threshold value, that is still grounds for suspicion, unless ruled out for other reasons.) An apparently abnormal plot may result when two adjacent dimensionalities have true minimum stress values which are almost equal. The values obtained may not quite reach the true value, of course, and the higher-dimensional one may fall short by a little more than the lower-dimensional solution, even though convergence is considered complete by the interpretation rules built into the program. The visible characteristics of this situation are that the higher-dimensional stress is very slightly higher than the lower-dimensional stress, usually a few units in the third decimal digit. Typically this occurs among two relatively high-dimensional solutions, where stress does not change much from one dimension to the next in any case.

If a stress value is suspiciously large, and convergence appears to be complete for this solution, the easiest way to check out the possibility of a local minimum is to obtain some more solutions in the same dimensionality, using different starting configurations. When the large stress value is due to a local minimum, it is usually possible to find a better solution with a nonsuspicious stress value in this way—if the data are at all suitable for analysis by MDS.

(5) The scatter diagram (which shows distance versus proximity value) should be examined for each solution, to see whether it exhibits the signs of a degenerate solution or looks abnormal in any way. For example, there is a type of abnormal behavior occurring only with metric scaling, in which the function f connecting dissimilarities and distances has the "wrong shape." If f is assumed to be linear, this could mean that f does not slope in the right direction (upward for dissimilarities, downward for similarities), or does not slope steeply enough. Such abnormal behavior indicates that a local minimum solution has been found.

Some Factors Affecting Stress

When considering stress values, it is important to remember that the interpretation of the values unfortunately depends on almost every possible choice or parameter available. In this section we give some guidelines to aid interpretation.

Never forget that the interpretation of stress values depends somewhat on the number of objects, I, and the dimensionality, R. As long as I is large compared to R, this effect is slight, and the exact values of I and R do not make much difference. As a rule of thumb, if $I > 4R$, the interpretation of stress is not sensitive to I and R. However, as I gets close to R, great changes occur. For example, in most situations a stress value of 0.02 indicates very good fit (though this may be vitiated by conditions we have discussed, such as degeneracy). On the other hand, for 7 objects in 3 dimensions, a stress as small as 0.02 or smaller will occur for contentless random data about 50% of the time (under "stress 1 ordinary conditions," as described below), and therefore is not small enough to indicate good fit. For 7 objects in 4 dimensions, a stress of 0 will occur well over 50% of the time, so even this best possible value of stress does not indicate good fit.

When numerical values of stress are discussed below, it is assumed (unless the contrary is indicated) that I is large enough relative to R so that the "ordinary" interpretation of stress is valid.

As a base for interpreting stress values, we define what is probably the most common set of conditions.

"Stress 1 ordinary conditions" or "Stress 2 ordinary conditions" imply:

- Nonmetric scaling (i.e., monotonic regression)
- Half matrix without diagonal

- No proximities missing (although a few missing proximities do not have much effect)
- No ties in the data (although a few ties in the data do not have much effect)
- Only one replication (that is, there is only one data value used for each proximity)
- Euclidean distances (i.e., the Minkowski r parameter has its usual value of 2)

Many rules of thumb for stress assume these conditions. Almost all of the statistical studies of stress which have been made to date use "ordinary conditions." (Some of these studies present significance tests for MDS. Unfortunately, the null hypothesis which all papers have used so far is unrealistic, and we do not recommend the routine use of such significance tests. However, the tables provided in these papers can provide a useful orientation if they are not interpreted too literally.)

Let us consider the effect of altering these conditions. (To explain the reasons behind these effects is not practical here.) It is always very important to know whether stress is being computed according to formula 1 or formula 2, since the numerical values for stress 2 are larger than those for stress 1. The use of metric scaling instead of nonmetric scaling has very little effect on the *configuration* in most cases (though it does occasionally), but it always increases stress, sometimes greatly.

Introducing the diagonal elements of the proximity matrix does not change the configuration, but it increases the stress, either slightly or moderately. Introducing the whole matrix of proximities (where δ_{ij} may be different from δ_{ji}) increases the stress, and increases it greatly if the δ_{ji} are often quite different from the δ_{ij}. Introducing replicated observations of the same proximity increases the stress, and will do so greatly if the replicated measurements are rather different from one another.

Unless there are a great many ties, their presence does not affect anything very much. The only common situation when there are so many ties that they have an effect is when the proximity values take on only a few distinct values.

Using Stress as a Guide to Dimensionality

If the precautions we previously mentioned have been effectively carried out, then it is reasonable to suppose that the stress values approximate the true minimum stress values for each dimensionality (as explained earlier in this section). Fortunately, the methods we discuss here provide a further check on departures from this situation.

Wherever specific numerical values for stress are mentioned, stress 1 ordinary conditions are to be understood. (Values of stress 1 below 0.20 under ordinary conditions can be roughly adapted to stress 2 ordinary conditions by multiplying by about 2 or 3.)

There are two basic approaches to the use of stress as a guide to dimensionality: one is statistical, the other is older and based on experience and intuition. Both approaches have value. The statistical approach requires less skill and is much less subjective; the intuitive approach is usable in a wider set of situations. The tables necessary for the statistical approach have only been published for ordinary conditions and for a limited range of values of I (the number of stimuli).

The statistical approach is explained fully in Appendix C. Here we simply give an extremely brief indication of its flavor. The given data are scaled in several dimensionalities and the stress plotted as a function of dimensionality, as shown for two sets of data in Figure 16. In principle, the plot consists merely of a few points, though it is conventional to connect these points by straight lines (dashed lines in the figure). Then this plot is compared with similar plots (shown by solid lines) derived by Monte Carlo techniques (i.e., simulation) for synthetic data in which the true dimensionality and the true error level are known. By finding the Monte Carlo plot which best matches the actual plot, we infer the dimensionality and error level of the actual data.

The older, intuitive approach for using stress values as a guide to dimensionality has many elements in common with the statistical approach, but experience and intuition rather than Monte Carlo calculations are the source of information. One simple observation is that if the true dimensionality R_t of the data is not 1, then the stress for $R = 1$ is almost always quite large. Roughly speaking, if the stress for $R = 1$ is below .15, this strongly suggests that $R_t = 1$ (assuming there are at least 10 stimuli).

If the error level e is small enough, then the plot will show an "elbow" at $R = R_t$ (unless $R_t = 1$). For example, see the Monte Carlo results for $R_t = 2$ in Figure 16. The sharpest possible elbow is apparent for e = 0; the best possible elbow one is likely to encounter in practice is seen for e = 0.06. With experience, one can just barely detect the elbow (at R = 2) for e = 0.12, though one would place little confidence in it; the curve for e = 0.25 has no elbow at all.

However, the visual sharpness of the bend must be interpreted in light of many other features, such as the stress value and R at the supposed elbow, and the number of points, I. We give a few rules of thumb, but of course they are very incomplete. An elbow should seldom be accepted if the stress there is above 0.10. (If the bend is sharp enough at such a large stress to strongly suggest an elbow, this is inconsistent with the implied error level, and the elbow may be due to incomplete convergence or a local minimum at the next higher dimensionality.) In general, the shape of a valid elbow depends

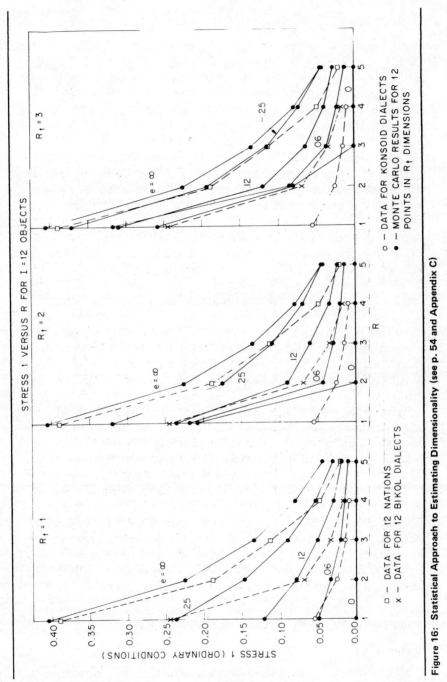

Figure 16: Statistical Approach to Estimating Dimensionality (see p. 54 and Appendix C)

on the stress at the elbow. For elbows at very small stress (such as 0.02), the right hand segment is very nearly horizontal, while the left hand segment need not be very steep. For elbows at quite large stress (say 0.10), the left hand segment is very steep but the right hand segment need not be very horizontal. Particular caution is needed for an apparent elbow at R = 2, since a very large stress at R = 1 has limited accuracy.

Elbows which meet the above tests are the exception rather than the rule. There are two reasons for this. For one thing, inequality among the principal components of a configuration (discussed on p. 91) takes away some of the bend at the elbow and distributes it among smaller values of R. For another, error tends to obscure everything, rounding off the elbow while raising the whole plot.

As a result, the plot frequently suggests a range of reasonable values for R_t. The rules of thumb are even vaguer here, and less trustworthy. The first and most important rule is that if stress values are nearly as large as those as for e = ∞, there is no point in attempting to estimate dimensionality statistically, and the use of MDS for these data is suspect. The plot for e = 0.25 and R_t = 2 has this character. Once we decide that stress is not that big, a weak elbow may be considered as one possible dimensionality. Beyond that, one is reluctant to suggest a dimensionality (other than 1) that yields stress much above 0.10. One hesitates to suggest a dimensionality larger than that needed to reduce stress to 0.05, unless each extra dimension reduces the stress substantially.

Applying the intuitive approach to the three examples on p. 90, the Konsoid data appears one-dimensional, and the Bikol data appears two-dimensional with a moderately good elbow. The 12 nations data have no elbow, but in accordance with the other considerations might appear four-dimensional. (They could even conceivably be five-dimensional. Whether we would want or dare to use four or five dimensions based on so few points is an entirely separate question.)

In some cases, a high error level can be reduced and the dimensionality more clearly indicated by suitable preprocessing of the data. The most important technique for this purpose is to take the squared Euclidean distances among the rows (or columns) of the proximity matrix and to analyze these transformed data by MDS (see Chapter 5 for further discussion).

OTHER CONSIDERATIONS CONCERNING DIMENSIONALITY

Interpretability

We previously mentioned three considerations in addition to goodness-of-fit that are important in choosing an appropriate dimensionality—interpretability, ease of use, and stability. In MDS, it is quite possible for (say) the two-dimensional configuration to have no interpretation, and yet for the three-dimensional configuration to have a full interpretation. This is possible because the relationship among configurations of different dimensionality is more complex than it is for other methods (see Appendix D).

Thus the way in which interpretability changes from one dimensionality to the next can be very complicated. However, interpretability often plays a central role in choosing the particular dimensionality within the range of reasonable dimensionalities suggested by goodness-of-fit. If the two-dimensional configuration has two or more interpretable directions, while the extra dimension in the three-dimensional configuration does not participate very much in any interpretation, then two dimensions should probably be used. Of course, the fact that the particular investigator cannot interpret a dimension does not necessarily mean that the dimension has no interpretation.

When the two-dimensional configuration does not resemble a perpendicular projection of the three-dimensional space, it may happen that no direction in the two-dimensional configuration is interpretable while one, two, three, or more directions in the three-dimensional space can be interpreted. In such a situation, three dimensions are needed to make sense out of the results.

For the purpose of interpreting a three-dimensional configuration, it is frequently helpful to discover what directions of projection, if any, makes it resemble the two-dimensional space; similar statements hold when more than three dimensions are involved. When visual inspection is not sufficient for discovering this direction, systematic statistical procedures can be used, e.g., linear regression, canonical correlation, and dimension (or factor) matching techniques.

Multiple regression can be helpful in choosing an appropriate dimensionality (see Appendix A). For example, if some variables (property vectors) have much higher multiple correlations in an $R + 1$ than in an R-dimensional configuration, then the higher dimensional solution is likely to be preferable. In practice, using one extra dimension beyond the dimensionality called for is sometimes desirable, since it may permit a cleaner interpretation of dimensions or of the configuration as a whole. (Similar advice is sometimes given for rotation in factor analysis.)

Regardless of dimensionality, if the configuration fits the data too badly, it may be dangerous to use. No apparent interpretations can be trusted, and real tendencies are likely to be obscured. Using more dimensions should always improve the goodness-of-fit, and using a large number of dimensions may avoid a very bad fit. On the other hand, when too many dimensions are used, the configuration adapts itself to the random error in the data, and this may actually make it more difficult to find the valid and interesting aspects. If these two considerations rule out all possible dimensionalities, the data may need to be handled differently, or may be unsuitable for MDS.

Ease of Use

Since it is generally easier to work with two-dimensional configurations than with those involving more dimensions, ease of use considerations are also important for decisions about dimensionality. For example, when an MDS configuration is desired primarily as the foundation on which to display clustering results, then a two-dimensional configuration is far more useful than one involving three or more dimensions. Even though a two-dimensional perpendicular projection of a higher dimensional solution can sometimes be used for this purpose, there may be an apparent lack of correspondence between MDS and clustering results due to the other dimensions. In some cases, this problem can be handled by using a new procedure by Carroll and Pruzansky (1975) that allows for multiple clusterings or "trees" (or combination of trees and dimensions). One set of clusters may fit nicely in a plane defined by two dimensions of the MDS space, while another set of clusters (based on a second tree) may fit into another plane of the configuration (see Carroll, 1976). In this regard, Carroll has suggested that a hierarchical clustering contains about the same amount of information as two dimensions from MDS.

It is not useful to examine only a configuration with so many dimensions that you cannot comprehend it. Higher-dimensional configurations are likely to be useful only when supplementary techniques are used to find comprehensible and interesting structures. Most often, these are directions in the configuration, but they can be planes, curves, neighborhoods, and other structures suggested by Guttman (1954). Thus, even when the data seem to call for a four-dimensional configuration, we may want to make use of the configurations in two and three dimensions as well; often this will facilitate the comprehension of the higher-dimensional configuration. Furthermore, if the most important and interesting aspects of a higher-dimensional space are already displayed in the two-dimensional configuration (see Shepard, 1974), then it may be desirable in some situations to use only the two-dimensional space. Besides being easier for the investigator to comprehend, it is far simpler to explain its meaning to most audiences. On the other hand, some important aspects of the structure are not always confined to the first two or three dimensions. In some cases, one may even find that the higher dimensions help to clarify the interpretation of the two-dimensional results. When this happens, the structure of the data may be obscured by trying to represent it in too few dimensions.

Stability and Related Considerations

The MDS configuration, like the data from which it is derived, is virtually always subject to substantial random variability. Even with reasonably good data, it is not unusual to find local minimum solutions which differ slightly from the best solution possible. One type of local minimum solution commonly observed can be obtained from the global minimum by the interchange of two nearby points, followed by slight accommodating motions of all the points. Less commonly, two separate pairs of points may be "flipped" in this way, or a more complex motion may occur for three or four nearby points. Real quantitative information on the size of such changes is scanty and quite complex, since the positions of nearby points are strongly interdependent. Therefore, we resort to a crude personal rule of thumb: in a typical situation, inferences should not be drawn that would change if several points were relocated by about 10% of the diameter of the configuration.

This brings up an important general consideration. It is a basic principle of inductive inference that we want to draw conclusions which are supported not only by the precise data observed, but also by many of the alternative data sets that could have reasonably occurred (in view of the random variability). This suggests the possible value of a procedure which in other contexts is called sensitivity analysis. If a particular set of data and the accompanying configuration are sufficiently important to warrant such an investigation, it is perfectly feasible to determine how sensitive the configuration is to changes in the data.

One simple way to assess the stability of the dimensions and other aspects of the configuration is to split the original data in several ways, and to do separate MDS analyses for each part. If enough subjects are involved, the splitting could be based on randomly selected subgroups. Likewise, stimuli could be eliminated from the data matrix, and solutions determined for the remaining stimuli using the "jacknife" idea of J. W. Tukey (Mosteller and Tukey, 1977). Another procedure is to produce several sets of alternative data by adding random variation to the given data in a realistic way. Greater confidence could be placed in dimensions and other features that are common to all the configurations.

Decisions about dimensionality can be based in part on such stability considerations. If R dimensions are stable across the various configurations, then an R-dimensional solution is warranted. Even though a dimension reduces stress very slightly, its consistency across configurations may be sufficient grounds for retaining it.

Going beyond stability to "generalizability," important considerations arise when we compare configurations based on different data collection methods. For example, the first two dimensions based on one method may resemble the third and fourth dimensions based on another method. If two-dimensional solutions were obtained for each data set, one might wrongly conclude that the results for different data collection methods have almost nothing in common. On the other hand, if the correspondence between the configurations is much greater on the first two than on the third and fourth dimensions, then using too low a dimensionality may lead to a conclusion that the results for the various methods are more similar than is justified by the data. In either case, a four-dimensional solution would provide a more accurate representation of the correspondence between results for those methods than a solution in fewer dimensions.

Before leaving the topic of dimensionality, one final point should be made. One does not get a dimension if the stimuli do not vary sufficiently on the associated attribute. Likewise, the stress reduction due to a dimension reflects its range of variation in the particular stimulus set, and not necessarily its relatively importance in general. It is, therefore, vital to be very careful to select stimuli so that there is sufficient variation on potential dimensions for them to have a chance to appear. More will be said about stimulus selection in an application discussed in the next chapter.

4. THREE-WAY MULTIDIMENSIONAL SCALING

INTRODUCTION

The type of MDS discussed in the previous chapters works essentially with only one matrix of proximities. Since a matrix is a two-way array, it is called two-way MDS. Suppose several matrices of proximities are available for the same objects, perhaps one from each subject. Although two-way MDS can analyze these data, it does so by treating the differences among the matrices as due to random error. Computer programs for two-way scaling include KYST, M-D-SCAL, TORSCA, and SSA, as well as others mentioned in the next chapter.

Three-way multidimensional scaling uses several matrices of proximities, which constitute a three-way array, and allows for large systematic differences among the matrices. The first method of this kind was three-mode multidimensional scaling (Tucker, 1964, 1972). Other methods of this kind include the INDSCAL model (Carroll and Chang, 1970a), the independently invented but virtually identical PARAFAC (Harshman, 1972), the points-of-view model (Tucker and Messick, 1963), and some others. Among three-way MDS methods of general interest at this time, only the INDSCAL-PARAFAC model exploits the differences among the several matrices to achieve a unique orientation of the axes, a fact which turns out to be of great practical value. For this reason, we limit our discussion to the use of this model. Comparison among these models may be found in Carroll and Wish (1974a, b). Computer programs of general interest for the INDSCAL model include the INDSCAL program and a newer program called ALSCAL (Takane, Young, and De Leeuw, 1976).

THE INDSCAL MODEL

The data for INDSCAL consist of several proximity matrices. Suppose there are K of them, and we index them by $k = 1$ to K. Let the proximities in matrix k be $\delta_{ij,k}$. In the most common situation, $\delta_{ij,k}$ indicates the dissimilarity or similarity between stimuli i and j as judged by person k. We shall often discuss the model using terminology appropriate to this situation, although there are many other possibilities. The proximities appropriate for the INDSCAL model are as general as those for the ordinary MDS model; we will not review the many possibilities again here. The K matrices may also represent different occasions on which the proximities are measured, different conditions under which they are taken, or proximities with respect to different characteristics.

Just as in two-way MDS, INDSCAL determines a configuration of points $x_1, \ldots, x_R$ called the "group stimulus space." (See Figure 17 for a very simple artificial example, in which there are $I = 4$ points and $K = 3$ subjects.) In addition, there is a set of K points $w_1, \ldots, w_K$ in another space called the weight space (or subject space), one point for each subject. This space and the points in it do not exist for ordinary MDS. In principle, the coordinates of points in the weight space should always be positive (or zero). In practice, the estimation procedures sometimes yield small negative values. (If these values are near 0, they reflect only statistical fluctuation; if substantial, they reflect some deviation between the model and the data. Very often it means that the dimensionality is too large for the data or that an inappropriate input option was used.)

The distances among the points of the group space are not used by INDSCAL. Instead, a new configuration is created for each subject k, and the distances in these configurations are used, as illustrated in Figure 17. A configuration for individual k is made by altering the group configuration space according to the weights in the weight vector w_k. Specifically, we stretch (or shrink) the first axis of the group configuration by $\sqrt{w_{k1}}$, the second axis by $\sqrt{w_{k2}}$, and so on, in order to obtain the kth individual's configuration.

Algebraically, the coordinates of the configuration for individual k are

$$\sqrt{w_{kr}}\, x_{ir}.$$

If the distance between points i and j in configuration k is indicated by $d_{ij,k}$, then

$$d_{ij,k}^2 = \sum_{r=1}^{R} (\sqrt{w_{kr}}\, x_{ir} - \sqrt{w_{kr}}\, x_{jr})^2$$

$$= \Sigma w_{kr}(x_{ir} - x_{jr})^2.$$

It is these distances which are used by the INDSCAL model.

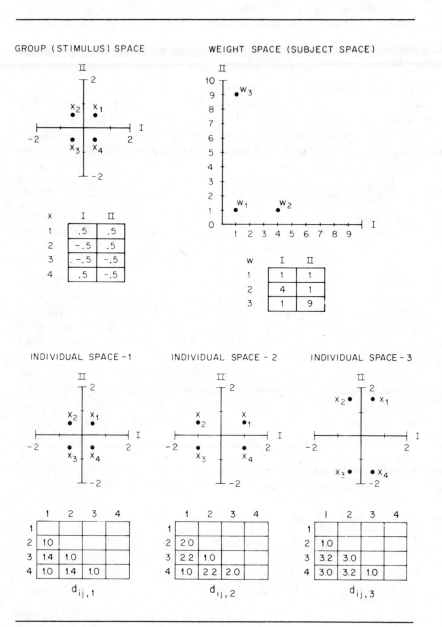

Figure 17: The Basic Concepts of the INDSCAL Model

We have described the $d_{ij,k}$ as distances in individual configurations, but another interpretation is possible. Looking at the equation for $d_{ij,k}$ we can say that these are the *weighted* Euclidean distances among the points of the *group* stimulus space rather than ordinary distances in the individual spaces. In this interpretation, the kth subject *weights* the squared coordinate differences $(x_{ir} - x_{jr})^2$ by the weights w_{kr}.

One central reason why the INDSCAL model is so useful in practice is that in most cases the interesting directions in the configuration are along the coordinate axes. If the positions of the axes are arbitrary (as in two-way MDS), then it is obvious that we cannot hope for them to have any special properties. The basic reason why the axes are determined uniquely with INDSCAL is that the stretching and shrinking is permitted only along the coordinate axes. Thus the coordinate axes play a special role which other directions do not. Although this does not mean that the unrotated axes from an INDSCAL analysis will necessarily have substantive meaning, the empirical fact is that they have been directly interpretable in most cases (see Wish and Carroll, 1974). Since this simplifies the interpretation of dimensions from INDSCAL, it is easier to work with higher dimensional solutions than when two-way MDS is used (see Appendix E for a comparison with other methods).

Determining dimensionality for INDSCAL solutions is somewhat different than the procedures we described for two-way scaling. There are many reasons for this: a different measure of fit is customary (percentage of variance accounted for, rather than stress); the dominant version of INDSCAL is metric, while the most widely used type of two-way scaling is nonmetric; there is a different background of experience; and there are no published tables.

While a systematic account of choosing dimensionality for INDSCAL is outside the scope of this paper, one significant point is worth noting. It sometimes happens that an additional dimension does not improve the overall percentage of variance accounted for by very much, but is used with high weights by a few subjects while irrelevant to most others. In this case, it is usually desirable to keep the dimension, particularly if the subjects using it are similar to each other in other ways.

INDSCAL ANALYSIS OF THE NATION SIMILARITIES DATA

In the previous examples, MDS solutions were obtained for the group as a whole by analyzing averaged data from all subjects. Invariably, these "group spaces" misrepresented the perceptual structures of some subjects. For example, matrices for two of the 18 subjects in the pilot study of nation perceptions are shown in Figures 18A and 18B. One subject (number 17) perceives all Communist countries to be alike and to be very different from non-

	BRZ	CON	CUB	EGY	FRA	IND	ISR	JPN	CHI	RUS	USA	YUG
BRAZIL												
CONGO	7											
CUBA	8	5										
EGYPT	2	7	6									
FRANCE	3	3	2	6								
INDIA	2	7	2	6	2							
ISRAEL	3	2	3	8	5	7						
JAPAN	2	1	1	4	3	7	2					
CHINA (MAINLAND)	2	6	8	7	4	5	3	7				
RUSSIA	2	3	7	7	3	6	3	6	8			
U.S.A.	5	3	3	4	8	5	7	8	1	2		
YUGOSLAVIA	2	2	8	3	4	5	4	6	8	8	2	

(A)   SUBJECT 17

	BRZ	CON	CUB	EGY	FRA	IND	ISR	JPN	CHI	RUS	USA	YUG
BRAZIL												
CONGO	6											
CUBA	8	6										
EGYPT	5	7	4									
FRANCE	3	3	2	2								
INDIA	4	5	3	3	3							
ISRAEL	3	4	2	5	4	3						
JAPAN	3	3	3	2	3	5	3					
CHINA (MAINLAND)	2	2	3	2	2	5	3	7				
RUSSIA	2	2	2	2	4	4	4	6	8			
U.S.A.	5	2	3	2	8	5	6	7	3	5		
YUGOSLAVIA	2	2	2	4	5	4	7	4	4	6	3	

(B)   SUBJECT 4

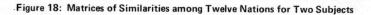

Figure 18: Matrices of Similarities among Twelve Nations for Two Subjects

Communist countries, while the other subject (number 4) has a very different "world view."

To illustrate INDSCAL, we apply the procedure to the set of 18 matrices (one per subject) from the previously discussed pilot study of similarities among 12 nations. (The KYST results for the data averaged across subjects are shown in Figure 8.) A detailed description of the results can be found in Wish (1971), and in Wish, Deutsch, and Biener (1970).

Although there is evidence that at least three dimensions are needed, it suffices for our illustrative purposes to focus on the two-dimensional INDSCAL solution. Stimulus coordinates on the *unrotated* dimensions are listed in Figure 19A and plotted in Figure 19B. As the figures show, these (unrotated) dimensions appear to have virtually the same meaning as those found previously by rotating the axes of the KYST solution. Thus, the dimensions can be interpreted as "Political Alignment" (or "Pro-Communist versus Pro-Western") and "Economic Development."

Statistical procedures can be used to compare the configurations from the INDSCAL and KYST analyses. Since the orientation of axes is different for these two configurations, one should not expect close correspondence between the unrotated dimensions of these two configurations. In this regard, the first KYST dimension (Figure 8B) correlates .64 with INDSCAL dimension 1, and .83 with INDSCAL dimension 2. The second KYST dimension correlates .73 and −.51, respectively, with the two INDSCAL dimensions. Agreement between results is much clearer when the *rotated* KYST dimensions (Dims. 1' and 2' in Figure 8C) are correlated with the *unrotated* INDSCAL dimensions. Here the correlations between corresponding dimensions are .99 for political alignment and .96 for economic development.

With only two dimensions, it is quite easy to see whether two multidimensional spaces agree. With more dimensions, however, one may fail to see the agreement between two highly related spaces that have differently oriented axes. The simplest way to determine if the dimensions from one space are included in the other space is to do multiple regression analyses, with one set of dimensions as independent variables (predictors), and each dimension from the other set as a dependent variable. This procedure will also show how one set of dimensions should be rotated to best match those from the other set. The two sets of dimensions can be compared by means of canonical correlation and factor matching procedures as well (see Cliff, 1966; Green and Rao, 1972; and relevant papers in this series).

Except for a difference in orientation and stretching of axes, the "group stimulus space" from INDSCAL is almost always very similar to the solution from a two-way MDS program. One can, therefore, often save computer time by using a KYST (or comparable) solution for averaged data as a starting configuration for the INDSCAL or ALSCAL programs.

The other important part of the INDSCAL computer output, the set of dimension weights, is shown in Figure 20A. It is often useful to relate these dimension saliences to other characteristics of the subjects. If other biographical or attitudinal information is available, one can investigate whether subjects who have high weights on a dimension differ from those with low weights on any of the background variables. Discriminant function analysis can also be used to distinguish groups with different patterns of dimension weights (see Jones and Young, 1972).

STIMULI	DIM. 1	DIM. 2
BRAZIL	.338	-.218
CONGO	.005	-.536
CUBA	-.341	-.253
EGYPT	-.089	-.272
FRANCE	.006	.235
INDIA	.189	-.271
ISRAEL	.306	.222
JAPAN	.219	.274
CHINA (MAINLAND)	-.449	-.055
RUSSIA	-.331	.297
U.S.A.	.407	.379
YUGOSLAVIA	-.321	.199

(a)

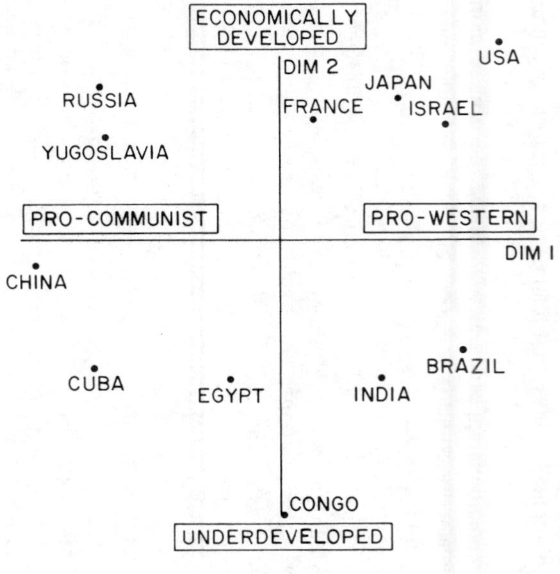

(b)

Figure 19: "Group Stimulus Space" from a Two-Dimensional INDSCAL Analysis of 18 Matrices of Similarities among Nations (one for each subject). The Coordinates are Listed in (a) and Plotted in (b).

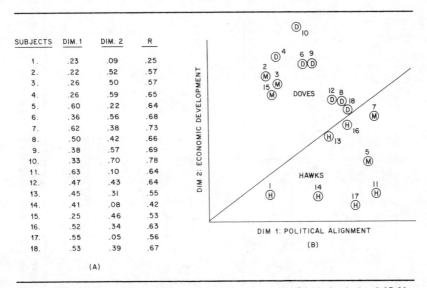

SUBJECTS	DIM. 1	DIM. 2	R
1.	.23	.09	.25
2.	.22	.52	.57
3.	.26	50	.57
4.	.26	.59	.65
5.	.60	.22	.64
6.	.36	.56	.68
7.	.62	.38	.73
8.	.50	.42	.66
9.	.38	.57	.69
10.	.33	.70	.78
11.	.63	.10	.64
12.	.47	.43	.64
13.	.45	.31	.55
14.	.41	.08	.42
15.	.25	.46	.53
16.	.52	.34	.63
17.	.55	.05	.56
18.	.53	.39	.67

(A)

DIM 1: POLITICAL ALIGNMENT

(B)

Figure 20: Dimension Weights from a Two-Dimensional INDSCAL Analysis of 18 Matrices of Similarities among Nations (one for each subject). The Weights are Listed in (a) and Plotted in (b), the "Subject Space."

Figure 20B graphically represents the dimension weights listed in Figure 20A. The D's, M's, and H's indicate whether the particular subject was classified as a "dove," "moderate," or "hawk" on the basis of an opinion item regarding the Vietnam war. The pattern of dimension weights can be seen to be quite different for hawks and doves; that is, the hawks give much more weight to political alignment than to economic development, while the reverse is true for the doves.

Figures 21A and 21B dramatize the difference between a hawk's eye and a dove's eye view of the world. These "private spaces" were obtained by applying the weights for subject 17 (a hawk) and subject 4 (a dove) to the respective dimensions of the group space (Figure 19). The extreme horizontal stretching of subject 17's space pushes the Communist and non-Communist countries far apart, and almost completely obscures the economic development dimension. The vertical stretching of subject 4's space results from the higher weight on the economic development dimension. (The original data for these two subjects are shown in Figures 18A and 18B, respectively.)

This example demonstrates how the INDSCAL model, like other three-way scaling models, can accommodate very large differences among individuals. Data for two subjects as different as those we have discussed can be fit into the same space even though the original matrices are almost completely uncorrelated. Although the INDSCAL model (like others for MDS) is an oversimplification, it goes a long way toward characterizing important variations in data structures.

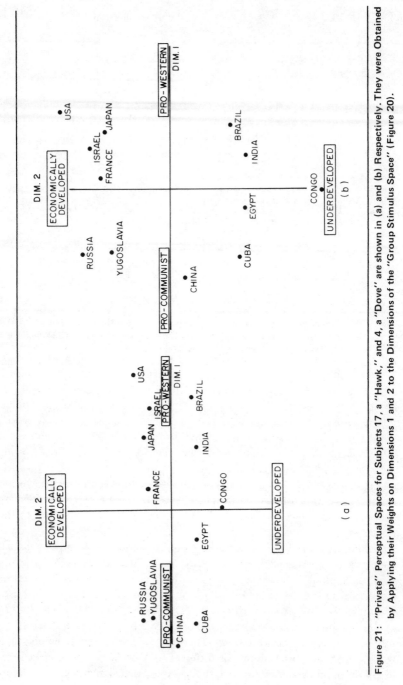

Figure 21: "Private" Perceptual Spaces for Subjects 17, a "Hawk," and 4, a "Dove" are shown in (a) and (b) Respectively. They were Obtained by Applying their Weights on Dimensions 1 and 2 to the Dimensions of the "Group Stimulus Space" (Figure 20).

Since these results are based on a very small sample, they should be regarded only as suggestive. However, more extensive studies involving more subjects and more nations replicated these results, and brought out additional information (see Wish, Deutsch, and Biener, 1970, 1972).

FITTING THE FRIENDSHIP RATINGS INTO
THE SIMILARITIES SPACE

In the previous example, we found the multidimensional space which best fit the set of similarity matrices and determined the dimension weights for each subject participating in the study. There are times, however, when the stimulus dimensions are known from prior investigations, and the only interest is to determine the dimension weights for a new group of subjects. There is a simple, inexpensive way to use the INDSCAL program for this purpose: the old configuration is used as a starting configuration, and the program is run for zero iterations. This keeps the stimulus dimensions fixed while solving for the dimension weights.

This option in INDSCAL is valuable for several purposes. For example, if one has several hundred subjects, it may be prohibitive to include all subjects in a single analysis. One could instead do an INDSCAL analysis on a sample, and then solve for the other subjects' weights by the above procedure. The use of a previously obtained configuration may also be desired in a longitudinal study, so that data from different time periods can be compared with respect to a common frame of reference. One could also do a separate INDSCAL analysis for the new data to see if the configuration itself had changed, or analyze the old and new data simultaneously.

The use of this zero iterations option in the INDSCAL program will now be illustrated for still another purpose. In this case we want to determine how important each dimension from the INDSCAL analysis of similarities among nations is when the same subjects rate the degree of friendship between pairs of nations. This amounts to using INDSCAL to perform a kind of multiple regression, where the independent variables are the stimulus dimensions shown in Figure 19, and the dependent variables are the 18 matrices of perceived friendship among nations.

Figure 22 shows the mean dimension weights for doves, moderates, and hawks derived from the friendship matrices, and compares their results with those previously obtained for the similarity ratings. Although the relative importance of dimensions differs strongly among these three subgroups for such similarity ratings, the three groups have virtually identical patterns of weights for the friendship ratings. This figure also shows that the doves and moderates change their dimension saliences according to the kind of judgment they are making, that is, the importance of economic development relative to political alignment is much less for their friendship than for their similarity ratings. In contrast, the relative importance of dimen-

	DIM. 1 POLITICAL ALIGNMENT	DIM. 2 ECONOMIC DEVELOPMENT	DIM. 2 / DIM. 1
A. FRIENDSHIP RATINGS			
DOVES	.61	.19	.31
MODERATES	.61	.19	.31
HAWKS	.59	.20	.34
B. SIMILARITY RATINGS			
DOVES	.40	.52	1.30
MODERATES	.39	.41	1.05
HAWKS	.47	.16	0.34

Figure 22: Mean Weights on Dimensions Based on INDSCAL Analysis of Similarity Ratings: (weights for friendship ratings determined by zero-iterations option in INDSCAL)

sions is the same for the hawks when they rate friendship as when they rate similarities among nations.

INDSCAL ANALYSIS OF PROFILE PROXIMITIES

In Chapter 1, we indicated that a rectangular matrix of, say, scales or individuals by stimuli, could be transformed into a square matrix of profile proximities between stimuli. For example, in a study by Rusk and Weisberg (1972), the original matrix indicated respondents' preferences among potential presidential candidates (as assessed by a "feeling thermometer"). Correlations between preferences for every pair of candidates were computed, and the correlation matrix was analyzed by two-way MDS (using M-D-SCAL).

In the process of computing correlations, any differences between means or standard deviations for the various stimuli are removed. Thus in the Rusk and Weisberg study, there could be a high correlation between preferences for two candidates, even if every respondent liked one and disliked the other (say, ratings of 90, 92, 94 versus 10, 12, 14). When one is only interested in the pattern of responses and wishes to remove level and variation effects, correlations or related measures should be used. On the other hand, when it is desirable to preserve the information about means and standard deviations, then the profile distance measure shown in Figure 23 is appropriate. (There are instances, however, when the level and variation differences are so great that information about the patterns is obscured in computing profile distances.)

In some studies, there are several such matrices referring to the same set of stimuli, e.g., one for each individual participating in a study, for each of several scales on which the stimuli are rated, or for various time periods when data are collected. If each of the original data matrices is transformed into a matrix of profile proximities, then the entire set of matrices can be analyzed by INDSCAL or other three-way methods. Examples are given in Wish and Carroll (1974) and Wish, Deutsch, and Kaplan (1976).

To clarify this procedure, let us assume that K persons have rated I stimuli on S rating scales. An I by I matrix of profile distances between stimuli can then be derived for each person and for each scale. Starting from an S by I matrix showing one person's ratings (see Figure 23A), where rows correspond to scales and columns to stimuli, a proximity matrix can be obtained by computing distances among the columns. Likewise, Figure 23B demonstrates how a proximity matrix can be derived for a single rating scale.

The set of K matrices for persons or S matrices for rating scales can be analyzed by the INDSCAL program.[6] In either case, the computer output indicates the stimulus coordinates on each dimension and a set of dimension weights for each matrix included in the input. When the matrices are associated with persons (one matrix per person), the situation is the same as in the previous examples, that is, a set of dimension weights is determined for each individual. When each matrix is derived from all subjects' ratings of the stimuli on a single scale, however, the dimension weights apply to the various rating scales. The higher the dimension weight for a rating scale, the more relevant the associated attribute is to the conceptualization of the dimension; or alternatively, the higher the weight, the more salient the particular dimension is when stimuli are rated on that scale.

Since the number of rating scales is usually far less than the number of subjects, it is more efficient to first analyze the set of matrices representing each scale, and then to use the zero iterations option (see the preceding example) to determine dimension weights for each person. In practice, this leads to clearer and more stable results because the reliability of values in a matrix representing all subjects' ratings of stimuli on one scale is higher than

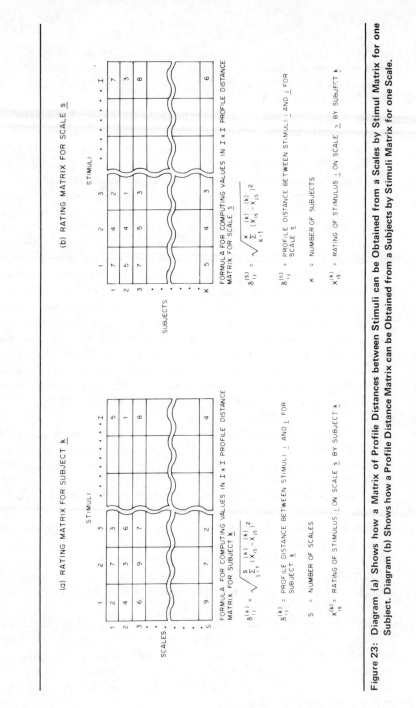

Figure 23: Diagram (a) Shows how a Matrix of Profile Distances between Stimuli can be Obtained from a Scales by Stimul Matrix for one Subject. Diagram (b) Shows how a Profile Distance Matrix can be Obtained from a Subjects by Stimuli Matrix for one Scale.

that for a matrix derived from one person's ratings of the stimuli on all scales. (When the number of individuals and scales is not too great or when there are no more than about 15 stimuli, it may be worthwhile to analyze the matrices for all individuals and scales simultaneously.)

Differences can occur between the spaces obtained from analyzing matrices for individuals and for rating scales. This may happen, for example, if some dimensions are represented by only a couple of scales, or if the standard deviations of original ratings are much smaller for scales measuring some dimensions than others. In such cases, the weaker dimensions may be washed out when profile distance matrices are computed for each individual. This problem can be reduced to some degree by normalizing ratings on each scale (e.g., by computing z-scores) prior to computing profile distances.

In all applications of MDS the results are, of course, dependent on the stimuli selected. When derived measures of proximity such as profile distances or correlations are used, the particular set of rating scales selected also has considerable influence on the dimensions themselves and on their relative importance. Thus, as in factor analysis, it is crucial to select a wide range of rating scales as well as stimuli when profile proximities are analyzed by INDSCAL.

5. PREPARING THE INPUT
FOR MULTIDIMENSIONAL SCALING

In this section, we discuss some of the practical choices which have to be made in the course of or on the way to actually applying MDS. A computer program must be chosen; in most cases the data need some form of preprocessing; and finally, certain decisions need to be made, such as whether to use metric or nonmetric scaling. Of course, these choices are all interrelated.

PREPROCESSING OF DATA

At several points, we have mentioned that some preprocessing of the original data may be desirable or necessary before applying MDS. Some of these steps are quite elementary, and some relate closely to certain options in using MDS. For example, if the data are already proximities, they must be arranged into a matrix, or into a lower or upper halfmatrix (with or without the main diagonal); suitable indication may also be needed to show which form is being used. If some proximities are missing and the program being used does not allow for this, a neutral value (such as the mean of the observed values) must be supplied. For KYST and M-D-SCAL (which do allow for missing proximities), an artificial value (smaller in the algebraic sense than any actual proximity) must be supplied for each missing proximity, and the CUTOFF phrase must be used to signal that these proximities are to be ignored. In some programs, the proximities may also be given different weights (to reflect greatly differing reliabilities if, for example, they are based on very different numbers of observations). If metric scaling is being used, the proximities may need to be transformed, as described later in the chapter. In this section, we mention some steps that can be taken prior to the MDS analysis which may make the data more appropriate for multidimensional scaling. Often such steps improve the goodness-of-fit and the interpretability of results.

Computing Profile Proximities

As mentioned in Chapter 1, for almost any kind of data, whether the entries are proximities or not, it may be sensible to form a matrix of proximities between the rows or the columns. The classical examples of this are provided by distances and correlations. This approach can be of value in a wide variety of situations.

Symmetrizing the Proximities

Although distances in an MDS configuration are necessarily symmetric (that is, $d_{ij} = d_{ji}$ for all i and j), the original proximities δ_{ij} may depart substantially from symmetry (that is, δ_{ij} may be quite different from δ_{ji}). When nonsymmetry in the proximities can be attributed primarily to unreliability, there are two natural alternatives. One is simply to use the nonsymmetric data matrix as input (many MDS programs will accept this); another is to "symmetrize" the proximities prior to using MDS, and then use only a half matrix. While the resulting configuration is usually almost the same either way, with symmetrizing the resulting goodness-of-fit values may be more helpful in choosing appropriate dimensionality. (Symmetrizing also reduces the computing time for MDS somewhat, by reducing the number of proximities.)

The simplest method of symmetrizing is to average δ_{ij} and δ_{ji}. This is usually quite adequate, though more elaborate methods have theoretical appeal in some cases (Shepard, 1974). An alternative approach is to compute an entirely new matrix of profile proximities, as described above.

Other Approaches to Nonsymmetric Proximities

Sometimes proximities are substantially nonsymmetric for systematic reasons. This is common for matrices where each row is associated with a stimulus and each column with a response. It is also common for "volume flow" matrices, where each row and column is associated with a country, city, or region, and each matrix entry indicates the volume of trade (or mail, telephone calls, etc.) from a sender (associated with the row) to a receiver (associated with the column). Journal inter-citation rates and sociometric choice matrices provide other examples, and many more could be given. Coombs (1964) refers to such matrices as "conditional proximity matrices," and contrasts their characteristics with those of symmetric proximity matrices.

The approaches described in the previous section ignore such nonsymmetry. While they are frequently useful even in the situations just described, they are theoretically unappealing. When the nonsymmetry is substantial, other approaches may not only be more appealing, but may in some cases give better results in practice. Sometimes it is sensible to preprocess the matrix of proximities by removing row effects and column effects (in the sense of analysis of variance), and this may greatly improve the symmetry. In effect, this replaces the original proximities with their interactions. In some situations, these may seem more appropriate than the original values.

An alternative approach for dealing with a nonsymmetric matrix is to split the matrix into its rows (or into its columns), and to allow for a different relationship between proximities and distances in each row (or column). This is especially useful for a matrix such as a conditional proximity matrix, where the proximities fall into separate groups in a natural way. For example, suppose the proximities are a sociomatrix, where each member of a group indicates on a rank order scale how friendly he or she is with each other member, and the ith row of the matrix gives the rank order values provided by member i. Since the entries are rank order indicators, it is more appropriate to use nonmetric scaling (though metric scaling might be used legitimately under certain circumstances). However, it is desirable to avoid making numerical comparisons between the entries in different rows, since these can be meaningful only with the aid of some additional assumptions, and nonmetric scaling (as previously described in this paper) rests on such comparisons.

To avoid this, imagine forming many scatter diagrams, one for each row of the matrix. In the ith scatter diagram we include only proximities from the ith row, namely, δ_{ij} for i fixed and j varying. In each scatter diagram, we approximate the points as well as possible by a different function f_i of the desired type (monotonic in this example), and use the stress to measure how far the scatter diagram is from displaying the desired relationship. We then pool these many different stress values into a single overall stress, and seek the configuration which optimizes the overall stress. The essential feature of this is that, rather than using one single function f for all the proximities, we permit several functions f_i, which may be very different from one another.

This particular variation of MDS may be accomplished in KYST and some versions of M-D-SCAL by an option called SPLIT-BY-ROWS, which splits the proximities into separate lists according to which row they are in, and performs a separate regression for each row.[7] It is perfectly sensible, in principle, to combine this option both with any type of metric or nonmetric scaling and with other options, and the programs mentioned permit such combinations. However, it should be remembered that some combinations are subject to particularly severe local minimum problems, so special precautions may be needed, such as using a good starting configuration obtained from some theoretically less appropriate but more robust variety of MDS.

METRIC VERSUS NONMETRIC MDS, AND TRANSFORMATION OF THE PROXIMITIES

The decision between metric and nonmetric scaling is not really a simple dichotomy, since the several varieties of metric scaling differ from each other as much as they do from nonmetric scaling. Furthermore, it is possible (using KYST or M-D-SCAL) to blend metric and nonmetric scaling in a "special combination" which offers certain advantages. (How to do this is described below.)

The choice of what kind of scaling to carry out is limited by the computer program being used, and that in turn is influenced by many obvious practical considerations such as easy availability, reliability of results, quality of documentation, and cost. Given a particular computer program, however, there may still be many alternatives, and the choice should reflect three major criteria: resistance to locally optimal solutions, resistance to degenerate solutions, and the degree to which the results aid in choosing the dimensionality.

Nonmetric scaling under "ordinary conditions" (described earlier) offers the greatest help in choosing dimensionality, for two reasons. First, this combination best resists misleading enlargement of the stress values due to an inappropriate assumption about the relationship between proximities and distances. Second, Monte Carlo studies are available and useful (see Appendix C). On the other hand, nonmetric scaling has far less resistance to degenerate solutions than most types of metric scaling, and has less resistance to locally optimal solutions than some forms of metric scaling.

Greatest resistance to local optima and to degeneracy is offered by classical multidimensional scaling and by a form of metric scaling available in KYST and M-D-SCAL (under the phrases REGRESSION=POLYNOMIAL=1, REGRESSION=NOCONSTANT), which attempts to make the distances in the configuration actually *proportional* to the proximities. Since both these methods are based on the idea that the proximities are proportional to distances, however, it is frequently necessary to preprocess the proximities to make this plausible. If the proximities are similarities, they must be "turned upside down" into dissimilarities, for example by forming

$$\text{dissimilarity} = \text{constant} - \text{similarity}$$

where the value of the constant is judiciously chosen. Dissimilarities may need to have a suitable constant added to them (in classical scaling, choosing this constant is called the "additive constant" problem). In some cases, a simple transformation such as taking the square root, squaring, or taking the logarithm, may be helpful. Fortunately, MDS is so robust a model (if there are enough data values relative to the number of coordinates being estimated, as discussed earlier) that such preprocessing does not need to be done very accurately. Because of the importance of such preliminary processing, the KYST program incorporates the ability to accomplish a considerable variety of such transformations prior to the scaling computation.

Where the preprocessing transformation seems difficult to choose accurately, it is helpful to permit a more flexible relationship between proximity and distance, such as permitting an intercept constant or using a higher degree polynomial (accomplished in KYST and M-D-SCAL by REGRESSION= CONSTANT and REGRESSION=POLYNOMIAL=1 or 2 or 3 for a linear, quadratic, or cubic polynomial). Unfortunately, this flexibility reduces the resistance to local optima and to degenerate solutions. To retain the flexibility and restore much of the resistance, it is possible in KYST and M-D-SCAL to blend metric and nonmetric scaling into a special combination. To do this, *two copies* of the same half matrix (or matrix) of proximities are entered, with the phrases for flexible metric scaling (like those just mentioned) given before the first copy, and either REGRESSION=ASCENDING or REGRESSION=DESCENDING, as appropriate, given before the second copy. Then the program computes and combines two stress values, and optimizes the combined stress: the first stress value by itself would correspond to metric scaling, the second by itself to nonmetric scaling.

Consider the ratio between the number of data values and the number of coordinates (stimuli x dimensions). We have already recommended that if this ratio is less than two, the configuration must be used very cautiously, if at all (see Chapter 2). If we are using halfmatrix without diagonal, and no proximities are missing or replicated, this ratio is $[I(I-1)/2]/IR = (I-1)/2R$. If the ratio is substantially larger, say four or more, then we have plenty of proximities, and we may expect the configuration to be robust. More precisely, almost the same configuration will almost always result from any reasonable assumption about f (i.e., the relationship between proximities and distances) in any number of dimensions which is reasonable for the data. (A prime example of an unreasonable assumption about f can occur inadvertently when using the program KYST with similarities. These require a *de*creasing relationship. If no explicit instruction is given to the program, it assumes an *in*creasing relationship by default. The resulting configuration has no meaning, but it frequently resembles one or several concentric circles or spheres.)

Where too many dimensions are used, the configuration may be fitting the noise, and is not at all stable. Slight changes of any kind, including a change in the type of function f, may have a great effect on the configuration. When too few dimensions are used, different possibilities may occur (as discussed in Chapter 3), and the choice of f may have an effect on which one occurs.

This robustness of configuration against changes in the function f is part of a more general robustness, which permits the configuration to be discovered even in the presence of substantial random error. This general robustness is one important reason for the practical success of MDS. It is also a reason why so many different methods of calculation can work successfully.

An important byproduct of this robustness is that a wrong choice of f can be discovered ex post facto. Regardness of what relationship we attempt to impose between the proximities and the distances, the points on the scatter diagram will display the actual relationship. For example, suppose we assume that distance is proportional to proximity, $f(\delta) = b\delta$ for some b. Then the fitted line will necessarily go through the origin on the scatter diagram. However, the points on the scatter diagram may clearly show a substantial intercept, which indicates that $f(\delta) = a + b\delta$ is more appropriate for the data.

However, note that it is only the *configuration* which is robust: the stress value is not. While an inappropriate assumption may inflate stress, possibly substantially, due to the phenomenon just described, the best choice of f is not necessarily the one which yields the smallest stress. In particular, non-metric scaling will almost always yield smaller stress than any metric scaling, but an appropriate type of metric scaling may yield a slightly more accurate configuration.

SOME AVAILABLE COMPUTER PROGRAMS FOR MDS

Information about available computer programs becomes outdated more rapidly than information about the underlying methods they incorporate, just as information about different makes of automobiles goes out of date more rapidly than the theory of internal combustion engines. For this reason, we shall only give broad, general information. We make no attempt at completeness in our listing, but try to include all programs which are generally available and widely used, as well as some other programs which seem of special interest for one reason or another (see Figure 24).

There have been several different major approaches to MDS. The first one is explained by Torgerson (1958), and uses the data values in a metric

NAME	EXPLANATION	AUTHOR(S)	SOURCE*
Two-Way Scaling Only			
M-D-SCAL	Multidimensional SCALing	Kruskal	Bell
TORSCA	TORgerson SCALing	Young	Thurstone
SSA-I through SSA-IV	Smallest Space Analysis	Guttman & Lingoes	Michigan
KYST	Kruskal Young Shepard Torgerson	Kruskal, Young & Seery	Bell or Thurstone
MRSCAL	MetRic SCALing	Roskam	Nymegen
MINISSA	Michigan Israel Netherlands Integrated SSA	Lingoes & Roskam	Michigan or Nymegen
MINITRI	Michigan Israel Netherlands Integrated TRIadic analysis	Roskam	Nymegen
Three-Way Scaling Only			
INDSCAL	INdividual Differences SCALing	Carroll & Chang	Bell
SINDSCAL	Small INDSCAL	Carroll & Pruzansky	Bell
PARAFAC	PARAllel FACtors factor analysis	Harshman	Western Ontario
3-Mode Scaling		Tucker & McCallum	Ohio State
Both Two-Way and Three-Way Scaling			
ALSCAL	Alternating Least-squares SCALing	Takane, Young & de leeuw	Thurstone

*See Figure 24(b) for full addresses.

Figure 24A: Computer Programs for MDS

BELL:

Computing Information Service
Attention: Mrs. Irma Biren
Bell Laboratories
600 Mountain Avenue
Murray Hill, New Jersey 07974

MICHIGAN:

Professor James C. Lingoes
1000A North University Building
The University of Michigan
Ann Arbor, Michigan 48104

NYMEGEN:

Professor Dr. Edw. E. Roskam
Department of Psychology
Erasmuuslaan 16
Nymegen, Holland

OHIO STATE:

Professor Robert McCallum
Department of Psychology
Ohio State University
Columbus, Ohio 43210

THURSTONE:

Thurstone Psychometric Laboratory
Attention: Professor Forrest Young
University of North Carolina
Chapel Hill, North Carolina 27514

WESTERN ONTARIO:

Professor Richard Harshman
Department of Psychology
University of Western Ontario
London 72, Ontario
Canada, N6A 5C2

Figure 24B: Sources for MDS Computer Programs

way. Unlike most other MDS procedures, this is not iterative. It was implemented by Young in a program called TORSCA. Subsequently, Young added a conceptually new feature to the program, which performed an iterative modification of the solution from the Torgerson method. By this means the program can accomplish a type of MDS that is substantially nonmetric, though not completely so in a mathematical sense. Still later, he added a second iterative procedure, closely modelled after the ideas and procedure in M-D-SCAL, to be carried out after the first one. TORSCA has gone through many different versions, several of which are still available.

The second major approach to MDS was initiated by Shepard, who created a program to accomplish a type of MDS which is substantially nonmetric in practice. His ideas were furthered and perfected by Kruskal, who created M-D-SCAL; this was the first program that carried out truly nonmetric scaling and embodied the idea of MDS based on systematic optimization of an objective function. This program has been available in several different versions. The latest available from Bell Laboratories is version 5 (M-D-SCAL 5 and 5M).

Subsequently, Young, Kruskal, and Seery combined the best features of TORSCA and M-D-SCAL into KYST. In essence, the Torgerson scaling procedure and Young's preliminary iterative procedure were integrated into M-D-SCAL.

A third major approach to MDS was due to Guttman, who prefers the name "smallest space analysis." This approach starts by using a procedure which has some similarity to Torgerson's, and then uses an iterative procedure which has some similarity to that used by Shepard. Lingoes implemented this method in a series of programs called SSA-I through SSA-IV. The same sorts of options which SSA provides through use of different versions of the program are available in some other programs through selection of options. Programs such as KYST and M-D-SCAL make much heavier use of options within the programs, while SSA tends to make use of alternate versions.

Later, Lingoes and Roskam created MINISSA, which is capable of carrying out MDS by all the procedures already mentioned. Originally, this program was created for the purpose of comparing different computational procedures. In its current version, it combines desirable features from several procedures and is practical for use with complete symmetric matrices. Roskam then created MRSCAL, which is the analogue of MINISSA, but for metric data.

Roskam also created another program, called MINITRI, which is designed especially to analyze triadic data. This type of data permits squared stress to be decomposed into two parts, in a manner very much like the analysis of variance, and this decomposition appears to help with the problem of deciding on the correct dimensionality (see Roskam, 1970). However, use of triadic data has the drawback of requiring a rather large number of data values, though this can be partially alleviated by using a balanced incomplete design.

INDSCAL was created by Carroll and Chang, who invented this method of carrying out individual differences scaling. It has been widely used because the method is very powerful, although the program uses considerable computer time. SINDSCAL is a streamlined version developed by Pruzansky. Harshman independently invented ideas very much like those of Carroll and Chang, and implemented them in a method and program called PARAFAC, the basic ideas of which give remarkable testimony to how similar independent inventions can be.

ALSCAL was created by Takane, Young, and De Leeuw. The method of analysis generalizes that of INDSCAL somewhat, and the program has some computational advantages. Unlike INDSCAL, this program can handle either two-way or three-way data, and does so by a single uniform approach.

NOTES

1. Some readers may wonder what happens to this definition if more than one configuration has the same smallest value of stress. In fact, this always occurs. However, these configurations are almost always effectively the same as one another, namely, they differ from each other by rigid motions such as rotation. In certain unusual situations there may be nonequivalent configurations with minimum stress, but even then they usually differ by so little that the uncertainty has no practical importance.

2. This is actually the principal axes orientation as provided directly by KYST. One can choose not to rotate to principal axes orientation if desired; normally, not rotating is useful only when a starting configuration obtained from some other analysis is used.

3. A four-dimensional analysis of data from a larger study replicated these results (Wish, Deutsch, and Biener, 1970, 1972). In addition to the dimensions of Figure 8, however, there were two others that reflected geographic and cultural proximities among nations.

4. The subjects were associates and friends of Kluver's organization, and do not in any sense comprise a random sample of the U.S. population.

5. Significance was determined by F-tests included in the computer output from the PROFIT program. There are R degrees of freedom for the numerator, corresponding to the number of dimensions. The degrees of freedom for the denominator of the F-ratio are I-R-1 (number of stimuli—number of dimensions—1).

6. When profile distances matrices are used, it is preferable to select the option of the INDSCAL program that reads the data values in as Euclidean distances rather than as dissimilarities. When the dissimilarities option is chosen, there are sometimes negative weights resulting from fitting of "noise" when additive constants are estimated. Options are also available in this program for reading in data as correlations or scalar products when appropriate.

7. Many other ways of splitting up the proximities are appropriate for different sorts of data, for example, by blocks or by replications. When data are collected by the method

of triads, one sensible way of analyzing them involves splitting the proximities into a separate list for each triad, so that each list contains only three proximities (see Roskam, 1970). Even more extensive splitting, so that each list contains only two proximities, is also possible (Johnson, 1973, and the "absolute value principle" of Guttman).

REFERENCES

BANKS, A. S. and GREGG, P. M. (1965) "Grouping political systems: Q-factor analysis of a cross-polity survey." Amer. Behavioral Scientist 9: 3-6.

BARLOW, R. E., BARTHOLOMEW, D. J., BREMNER, J. M., and BRUNK, H. D. (1972) Statistical Inference under Order Restrictions: The Theory and Application of Isotonic Regression. New York: John Wiley.

BLACK, P. (1977) "Multidimensional scaling applied to linguistic relationships," in I. Dyen (ed.) Lexicostatistics in Genetic Linguistics II: Proceedings of the Montreal Conference. Louvain, Belgium: l'Institut de Linguistique.

BOLLEN, A., CEDERGREN, R. J., SANKOFF, D. and LAPALME, G. (1974) "Spatial configuration of ribosomal proteins: a computer-generated model of the 30S subunit." Biochemical and Biophysical Research Communications 59 (3): 1069-1078.

CARROLL, J. D. (1976) "Spatial, non-spatial and hybrid models for scaling." Psychometrika 41: 439-463.

――― and CHANG, J. J. (1970a) "Analysis of individual differences in multidimensional scaling via an N-way generalization of 'Eckart-Young' decomposition." Psycho- metrika 35: 283-319.

――― (1970b) "A 'quasi-nonmetric' version of INDSCAL, a procedure for individual differences in multidimensional scaling." Paper presented at meetings of the Psychometric Society, Stanford, Cal.

CARROLL, J. D. and PRUZANSKY, S. (1975) "Fitting of hierarchical tree structure (HTS) models, mixtures of HTS models, and hybrid models, via mathematical programming and alternating least squares," pp. 9-19 in Theory, Methods, and Applications of Multidimensional Scaling and Related Techniques: Proceedings of the U.S.- Japan Seminar on Multidimensional Scaling. Tokyo: Japan Society for the Promotion of Science.

CARROLL, J. D. and WISH, M. (1974a) "Multidimensional perceptual models and measurement methods," pp. 391-447 in E. C. Carterette and M. P. Friedman (eds.) Handbook of Perception, vol. 2. New York: Academic Press.

――― (1974b) "Models and methods for three-way multidimensional scaling," pp. 57- 105 in D. H. Krantz, R. C. Atkinson, R. D. Luce and P. Suppes (eds.) Contemporary Developments in Mathematical Psychology, vol. 2. San Francisco: W. H. Freeman.

CHANG, J. J. and CARROLL, J. D. (1972) "How to use INDSCAL, a computer program for canonical decomposition of N-way tables and individual differences in multidimensional scaling." Bell Laboratories (unpublished).

――― (1968) "How to use PROFIT, a computer program for property fitting by optimizing nonlinear or linear correlation." Bell Laboratories (unpublished).

CLIFF, N. (1966) "Orthogonal rotation to congruence." Psychometrika 31: 33-42.

COOMBS, C. H. (1964) "A Theory of Data. New York: John Wiley.

GRAEF, JED and IAN SPENCE (1976) "Using prior distance information in multidimensional scaling." Paper presented at Joint Meeting of the Psychometric Society and Mathematical Psychology Group, Bell Laboratories, Murray Hill, N.J. (April).

GREEN, P. E. and RAO, V. R. (1972) Applied Multidimensional Scaling: A Comparison of Approach and Algorithms. New York: Holt, Rinehart and Winston.

GUTTMAN, L. (1971) "Measurement as a structural theory." Psychometrika 36: 329-347.

――― (1968) "A general nonmetric technique for finding the smallest coordinate space for a configuration of points." Psychometrika 33: 469-506.

――― (1966) "Order analysis of correlation matrices," pp. 438-458 in R. B. Cattell (ed.) Handbook of Multivariate Experimental Psychology. Chicago: Rand McNally.

――― (1965) "The structure of interrelations among intelligence tests," pp. 25-36 in Proceedings of the 1964 Invitational Conference on Testing Problems. Princeton, N.J.: Educational Testing Service.

――― (1954) "A new approach to factor analysis: the radex," pp. 258-348 in P. F. Lazarsfeld (ed.) Mathematical Thinking in the Social Sciences. New York: Free Press.

HARSHMAN, R. A. (1972) "PARAFAC2: mathematical and technical notes," in Working Papers in Phonetics 22, University of California at Los Angeles.

――― (1970) "PARAFAC: foundations of the PARAFAC procedure: models and conditions for an 'explanatory' multi-modal factor analysis." Working Papers in Phonetics 16, University of California at Los Angeles.

HAYASHI, CHIKIO (1974) "Minimum dimension analysis: one of the methods of multidimensional quantification." Behaviormetrika: 1-24.

――― (1961) "Sample survey and theory of quantification." Bulletin of the International Statistical Institute 38 (Part IV): 505-514.

――― (1954) "Multidimensional quantification, with the applications to analysis of social phenomena." Annals of the Institute of Statistical Mathematics 5(2): 121-143.

――― (1952) "On the prediction of phenomena from qualitative data and quantification of qualitative data from the mathematico-statistical point of view." Annals of the Institute of Statistical Mathematics 2: 69-98.

ISAAC, P. D. and POOR, D.D.S. (1974) "On the determination of appropriate dimensionality in data with error." Psychometrika 39: 91-109.

JOHNSON, RICHARD M. (1973) "Pairwise nonmetric multidimensional scaling." Psychometrika 38: 11-18.

JOHNSON, S. C. (1967) "Hierarchical clustering schemes." Psychometrika 32: 241-254.

JONES, L. E. and YOUNG, F. W. (1972) "Structure of a social environment: longitudinal individual differences scaling of an intact group." J. of Personality and Social Psychology 24: 108-121.

KELLER, F. S. and TAUBMAN, R. E. (1943) "Studies in International Morse Code. 2. Errors made in code reception." J. of Applied Psychology 27: 504-509.

KELLY, G. A. (1955) A Theory of Personality: The Psychology of Personal Constructs. New York: W. W. Norton.

KRUSKAL, J. B. (1976a) "Multidimensional scaling and other methods for discovering structure," in Enslein, Ralston, and Wilf (eds.) Statistical Methods for Digital Computers. New York: John Wiley (1977).

――― (1976b) "More factors than subjects, tests, and treatments: an indeterminacy theory for canonical decomposition and individual differences scaling." Psychometrika 41: 281-293.

――― (1964a) "Multidimensional scaling by optimizing goodness of fit to a nonmetric hypothesis." Psychometrika 29: 1-27.

――― (1964b) "Nonmetric multidimensional scaling: a numerical method." Psychometrika 29: 115-129.

KRUSKAL, J. B. and CARMONE, F. (undated) "How to use M-D-SCAL (Version 5M) and other useful information." Bell Laboratories (unpublished).

KRUSKAL, J. B. and CARROLL, J. D. (1969) "Geometric models and badness-of-fit functions," pp. 639-670 in P. R. Krishnaiah (ed.) Multivariate Analysis, vol. 2. New York: Academic Press.

KRUSKAL, J. B., YOUNG, F. W., and SEERY, J. B. (1973) "How to use KYST, a very flexible program to do multidimensional scaling and unfolding." Bell Laboratories (unpublished).

LINGOES, J. C. (1973) The Guttman-Lingoes Nonmetric Program Series. Ann Arbor, Mich.: Mathesis Press.

LINGOES, J. C. and GUTTMAN, L. (1967) "Nonmetric factor analysis: a rank reducing alternative to linear factor analysis." Multivariate Behavioral Research 2: 485-505.

MOSTELLER, F. and TUKEY, J. W. (1977) "Data analysis and regression: a second course in statistics." Reading, Mass.: Addison-Wesley.

OSGOOD, C. E., SUCI, G., and TANNENBAUM, P. H. (1957) The Measurement of Meaning. Urbana: Univ. of Illinois Press.

PRUZANSKY, S. (1975) "SINDSCAL: a computer program for individual differences in multidimensional scaling." Bell Laboratories (unpublished).

RICHARDSON, M. W. (1938) "Multidimensional psychophysics." Psychological Bulletin 35: 659-660.

ROSENBERG, S. and KIM, M. P. (1975) "The method of sorting as a data-gathering procedure in multivariate research." Multivariate Behavioral Research 10: 489-502.

ROSENBERG, S., NELSON, C., and VIVEKANANTHAN, P. S. (1968) "A multidimensional approach to the structure of personality impressions." J. of Personality and Social Psychology 9: 283-294.

ROTHKOPF, E. Z. (1957) "A measure of stimulus similarity and errors in some paired-associate learning tasks." J. of Experimental Psychology 53: 94-101.

ROSKAM, E. (1970) "Method of triads for nonmetric multidimensional scaling." Psychologie 25: 404-417.

RUMMEL, R. J. (1969) "Some empirical findings on nations and their behavior." World Politics 21: 226-241.

RUSK, J. G. and WEISBERG, H. F. (1972) "Perceptions of presidential candidates: Implications for electoral change." Midwest J. of Political Science 16: 388-410.

SAWYER, J. (1967) "Dimensions of nations: size, wealth, and politics." Amer. J. of Sociology 73: 145-172.

SEASHORE, H. and KURTZ, A. K. (1944) "Analysis of errors in copying code." Office of Scientific Research and Development, Report No. 4014.

SHEPARD, R. N. (1974) "Psychological representation of speech sounds," in E. E. David and P. B. Denes (eds.) Human Communication: A Unified View. New York: McGraw-Hill.

——— (1972) "A taxonomy of some principal types of data and of multidimensional methods for their analysis," pp. 21-47 in R. N. Shepard, A. K. Romney and S. Nerlove (eds.) Multidimensional scaling: Theory and Applications in the Behavioral Sciences, vol. 1. New York: Seminar Press.

——— (1963) "Analysis of proximities as a technique for the study of information processing in man." Human Factors 5: 33-48.

——— (1962) "The analysis of proximities: multidimensional scaling with an unknown distance function." Psychometrika 27: 125-140, 219-246.

SHEPARD, R. N. and KRUSKAL, J. B. (1975) "A nonmetric variety of linear factor analysis." Psychometrika 39: 123-157.

SLATER, P. B. (1976) "Hierarchical internal migration region of France." IEEE Transactions on System, Man, and Cybernetics 6: 321-324.

SPENCE, IAN (1972) "An aid to the estimation of dimensionality in nonmetric multidimensional scaling." Univ. of Western Ontario Research Bulletin No. 229.

SPENCE, IAN and GRAEF, JED (1974) "The determination of the underlying dimensionality of an empirically obtained matrix of proximities." Multivariate Behavioral Research 9: 331-342.

——— (1973) "How to use M-SPACE, a program for the determination of the underlying dimensionality of an empirically obtained matrix of proximities." Univ. of Western Ontario Research Bulletin No. 257.

SWADESH, M. (1952) "Salish phonologic geography." Language 28: 232-248.

——— (1950) "Salish internal relationships." Int. J. of Amer. Linguistics 16: 157-167.

TAKANE, Y., YOUNG, F. and DE LEEUW, J. (1976) "Nonmetric individual differences multidimensional scaling: an alternating least squares method with optimal scaling features." Psychometrika 42: 7-67.

TORGERSON, W. S. (1958) Theory and Methods of Scaling. New York: John Wiley.

TUCKER, L. R. (1972) "Relations between multidimensional scaling and three-mode factor analysis." Psychometrika 37: 3-27.

——— (1964) "The extension of factor analysis to three-dimensional matrices," pp. 109-127 in N. Fredriksen, and H. Gulliksen (eds.) Contributions to Mathematical Psychology. New York: Holt, Rinehart and Winston.

TUCKER, L. R. and MESSICK, S. (1963) "An individual differences model for multidimensional scaling." Psychometrika 28: 333-367.

WAGENAAR, W. A. and PADMOS, P. (1971) "Quantitative interpretation of stress in Kruskal's multidimensional scaling technique." British J. of Mathematical and Statistical Psychology 24: 101-110.

WEISBERG, H. F. and RUSK, J. G. (1970) "Dimensions of candidate evaluation." Amer. Political Science Review 64: 1167-1185.

WISH, M. (1976) "Comparisons among multidimensional structures of interpersonal relations." Multivariate Behavioral Research 11: 297-327.

——— (1975) "Role and personal expectations about interpersonal communication," pp. 69-77 in Theory, Methods, and Applications of Multidimensional Scaling and Related Techniques: Proceedings of the U.S.-Japan Seminar on Multidimensional Scaling. Tokyo: Japan Society for the Promotion of Science.

——— (1972) "Notes on the variety, appropriateness, and choice of proximity measures." Bell Laboratories (unpublished).

——— (1971) "Individual differences in perceptions and preferences among nations," 312-328 in C. W. King and D. Tigert (eds.) Attitude Research Reaches New Heights. Chicago: American Marketing Association.

——— (1970) "Comparisons among multidimensional structures of nations based on different measures of subjective similarity." General Systems 15: 55-65.

——— (1967) "A model for the perception of Morse code like signals." Human Factors 9: 529-539.

WISH, M. and CARROLL, J. D. (1974) "Applications of individual differences scaling to studies of human perception and judgment," pp. 449-491 in E. C. Carterette and M. P. Friedman (eds.) Handbook of Perception, vol. 2. New York: Academic Press.

WISH, M., DEUTSCH, M., and BIENER, L. (1972) "Differences in perceived similarity of nations," pp. 289-313 in A. K. Romney, R. N. Shepard, and S. Nerlove (eds.) Multidimensional Scaling: Theory and Applications in the Behavioral Sciences, vol. 2. New York: Seminar Press.

——— (1970) "Differences in conceptual structures of nations: an exploratory study." J. of Personality and Social Psychology 16: 361-373.

WISH, M., DEUTSCH, M., and KAPLAN, S. J. (1976) "Perceived dimensions of interpersonal relations. Journal of Personality and Social Psychology 33: 409-420.
WISH, M., and KAPLAN, S. J. (1977) "Toward an implicit theory of interpersonal communication." Sociometry 40: 234-246.
YOUNG, G. and HOUSEHOLDER, A. S. (1938) "Discussion of a set of points in terms
of their mutual distances." Psychometrika 3: 19-22.

APPENDIX A

Some Comments on Multiple Linear Regression

Linear (multiple) regression has an important geometical interpretation as picking out a particular direction in space. Closely associated with this is the multiple correlation coefficient, which plays an important role in linear regression. To explain both of these, we use a two-dimensional configuration (Figure 25). To describe the direction of a line L in the space we make use of *direction cosines* c_1, c_2, etc., which are defined by

$$c_r = \text{the cosine of the angle between L and the } r^{th}$$
$$\text{coordinate axis}$$

With any coefficients a, b_1, b_2, etc., there is associated a line L in a particular direction, namely, the direction for which the direction cosines satisfy

$$c_r = b_r \left/ \sqrt{b_1^2 + b_2^2 + \dots} \right.$$

(The coefficient *a* does not yet enter at this point.) For any point x_i, consider the perpendicular projection of x_i on L. The expression

$$a + b_1 x_{i1} + b_2 x_{i2} + \dots$$

gives the position of the perpendicular projection along L (with respect to some suitably chosen zero point and some suitable scale on L). We shall in-dicate this expression, and the position along L, by x_{iL}. The ordinary correla-tion coefficient between x_{iL} and the v_i is a measure of how well the points projected onto L fit v. Linear regression not only minimizes the sum of squares shown on p. 36, it also chooses a direction for L which maximizes the correlation coefficient. The resulting maximum value is in fact the multiple correlation coefficient between v and the R dimensions of the space. In other words, the multiple correlation coefficient is the ordinary correlation between v (the variable) and a weighted combination of the dimensions, using weights which maximize this correlation.

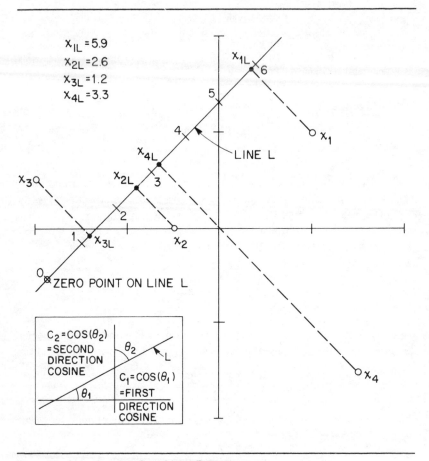

Figure 25: Some Concepts from Linear Regression

APPENDIX B

Other Uses for Lines and the "Horseshoe" Phenomenon

We have seen in a previous section how lines may be drawn on a configuration to help interpret and clarify neighborhoods. Lines connecting the points may be used for several other purposes as well. One of the most notable is to discover the "horseshoe" phenomenon, closely related to Guttman's "circumplex" idea, which is not uncommon and an important matter in itself.

Consider Figure 15, which is a configuration of 19 Salish dialects, on which lines have been drawn, one connecting each pair of points whose raw similarity is greater than 0.30. (Figure from Black, 1977; data due to Swadesh,

1950, 1952.) Although these data are two-dimensional in the sense of MDS, it is apparent that the two-dimensional configuration has a special character: it consists of a nearly one-dimensional configuration which has been bent around into a horseshoe shape. Only one curvilinear dimension is sufficient to give a reasonable description of them, namely, position of each dialect along the horseshoe (though a second coordinate, giving perpendicular distance from the nearest point on curved line of the horseshoe, would of course improve the description). The horseshoe phenomenon, which has been observed on quite a few occasions, is not entirely understood, but some conditions which can cause it are known. When it occurs, position along the horseshoe is another significant candidate for interpretation, along with directions in the space.

Lines between the points are a simple data analysis technique which could be used for a variety of purposes. One interesting application occurs in Shepard (1963), where the large similarities from Seashore-Kurtz data (1944) on Morse code errors by highly trained operators are shown by lines on the configuration from Keller-Taubman data (1943) on intermediate students. This permits an interesting comparison between the two sets of data which would be difficult to accomplish by other means, because the Seashore-Kurtz data has been recorded in too abbreviated a way to be used as input for MDS.

Other special structures may be revealed by lines corresponding to the larger raw similarities. Unfortunately, locating the large similarities and drawing these lines by hand is very tedious if there are many points. A computer facility to draw the lines on the configuration would be desirable; as an aid to hand drawing, such computer programs as KYST and M-D-SCAL already can print out the similarities in order of size. It is quite possible that curved lines and/or surfaces occur in three-dimensional or higher-dimensional configurations. Most likely they have not been observed because they are hard to see even if present.

APPENDIX C

Statistical Guide to Dimensionality

The statistical approach is based on the idea that there is a true underlying configuration in some dimensionality which we shall call R_t (t for "true"). It is assumed that the proximities are generated from the distances in the true configuration, but with random error of some kind incorporated at a controlled level e, and perhaps with monotonic distortion incorporated. When the proximities are scaled in several different dimensionalities, the plot of stress versus R depends primarily on R_t and e. Thus each combination of R_t and e corresponds to a particular appearance of the plot. Using a Monte Carlo approach, many configurations are generated and scaled, and in effect the plots are catalogued according to the (R_t,e) value.* The plot for our actual data is compared with the catalogue, and the values of R_t and e are inferred to be those which give a plot most like the one we have. If the plot is very different from any of the catalogued plots, this could be due to incomplete convergence or to a local minimum solution (in one or more dimensionalities). However, stress for R = 1 is particularly variable. (Also, there is a problem discussed below concerning unequal principal components.)

It is obvious that a large error level obscures all other features of data. This shows up in the fact that as e gets larger, the plots for different values of R_t look more alike (see Figure 16, Monte Carlo results for I = 12 objects). In the limit as e becomes infinite, they are identical. Thus we must expect that the larger e is, the less well is it possible to determine R_t.

Figure 16 illustrates this approach, using Monte Carlo results from Spence (1972) for the case of I = 12 objects. (Note that a very similar published version of this paper, Spence and Graef, 1974, does not contain the vital tables.) To use this technique for other values of I, a similar plot must be made for each desired value; Spence and Graef (1974) cover the case from I = 12 to I = 36. Data on 12 Konsoid dialects spoken in Ethiopia (Black, 1977) have stress .056, .026, .015, and .009 for R = 1,2,3,4 respectively, and are clearly one-dimensional. To see this, we note that the plot for these data closely matches the plot for R_t = 1 and e = 0.06 point by point, but is slightly below it. (This yields not only that R_t = 1, but also that e is slightly smaller than 0.06). According to this technique, the data cannot be two-dimensional or three-dimensional because the plots for R_t = 2 and 3 are very different from the Konsoid plot, in the sense that the stress values for the first one or two values of R are much too large.

Data on 12 Bikol dialects spoken in the Philippines (data from McFarland, quoted in Black, 1977) have stress .246, .069, .035, and .018 for R = 1,2,3,4 respectively, and appear to be two-dimensional. According to the technique, they cannot be one-dimensional, as we see in the plots for R_t = 1, because the stress for R = 1 is too large; nor can they be three-dimensional, as we see in the plots for R_t = 3, because the stress for R = 1 and 2 is too small. In the plots for R_t = 2, the Bikol plot drifts from slightly above e = 0.12 to slightly below 0.06, so the error level is probably intermediate between these values. It is not clear what causes the drift.

Data on 12 nations which were discussed earlier in this paper (see Figure 16) have stress .388, .187, .112, .049, and .022 for R = 1,2,3,4,5 respectively,

---

*"Monte Carlo" refers to repeated computer simulation using random numbers.

and present a less clear-cut result. It is obvious that the error level is much higher for these data than the preceding examples, whatever their dimensionality, and as we noted earlier this makes determination of dimensionality much less distinct if possible at all. (These data are based on ratings by only 18 subjects in a pilot study.) However, making use of the plots for $R_t = 4$ (not included here) and assuming that a drift like that above is acceptable, these data could be four-dimensional, with the plot drifting from e = .25 down to below e = .12. We reach this conclusion very hesitantly, since the stress values are so high. Indeed, if it were not for the relatively small stress at R = 4 and 5, then the stress alone might suggest that the data are too noisy to be any use at all. In general, it is the values of stress for R at or near the apparent true dimensionality which are most informative. As we have noted elsewhere, a configuration of so few points in so many dimensions may not be very well determined; we would only use the four-dimensional configuration with great caution, and even the three-dimensional configuration is marginal. It should be pointed out that in a larger study involving 75 subjects and 21 nations (Wish, Deutsch, and Biener, 1970, 1972) the configuration was clearly shown to be four-dimensional; and the dimensions there correspond reasonably well with those obtained from a four-dimensional analysis of the data discussed here.

Other ways of using catalogued plots are available (Wagenaar and Padmos, 1971; Spence and Graef, 1973 and 1974; Isaac and Poor, 1974). The method of Spence and Graef, which is available in a portable computer program called M-SPACE, appears to be the most useful statistical approach yet published. When this program was applied to the three sets of data above, it yielded the same dimensionalities stated above. Interpreting the supplementary output, Spence reported (private communication) that the Konsoid data are "one-dimensional—no question," that the Bikol data "is a pretty clear two-dimensional data set," and that the 12 nations data is hard to decide: "it either really is of high dimensionality or there is excessive noise and the structure is unreliable." Only external information such as the later more extensive data set referred to above permits us to decide that the former possibility is correct.

All the statistical methods published so far suffer from limitations, so their results should be considered tentative. It was stated above that stress depends primarily on R_t and e. This oversimplification is one limitation. While the exact nature of the configuration in R_t dimensions does not appear to have much effect on stress, the relative size of its principal components has an effect. Spence, as well as Wagenaar and Padmos, use configurations for which all factors or dimensions are about equally important. The main practical consequence for the Spence method is that a configuration which has (say) two strong dimensions and one moderate dimension will appear to be intermediate between $R_t = 2$ and 3. If the third dimension is small rather than moderate, the Spence method may deny it entirely, although interpretability and stability over different data sets may support its reality. Isaac and Poor use a rather different ad hoc approach, which is intrinsically limited.

APPENDIX D

Relationship Between MDS Solutions in Different Dimensionalities

In principal components analysis, the configuration in $R - 1$ dimensions can be obtained from the configuration in R dimensions by dropping the last coordinate, and somewhat the same situation exists in factor analysis. In MDS the situation is usually more complicated. With the exception of a particular procedure for MDS presented by Torgerson (1958), the above statement is never precisely true for MDS. However, something like it is often approximately correct.

Dropping the last coordinate from a two dimensional configuration is the same as projecting it perpendicularly onto the horizontal axis. In MDS, the one-dimensional configuration can often be obtained to an approximation by projecting it perpendicularly onto *some* line in the two-dimensional space. In some cases, however, the one-dimensional configuration is obtained to an approximation by unbending a curve through the two-dimensional configuration; in other cases, no systematic relationship may be apparent between the two configurations.

Dropping the last coordinate from a three-dimensional configuration is the same thing as projecting it perpendicularly onto the plane of the first two coordinates. In MDS, the two-dimensional configuration can sometimes be obtained to an approximation by projecting the three-dimensional configuration perpendicularly onto *some* plane. However, this need not be the case. Similar statements may be made for higher-dimensional configurations as well.

APPENDIX E

Determining Meaningful Directions by INDSCAL and by Other Methods

A comparison of the INDSCAL model with principal components analysis is instructive. Either with the configuration provided by ordinary MDS, or with a configuration of directly observed data points, the calculation of principal components provides directions which are determined by the data (given certain mathematical assumptions). Thus it is also possible for these directions to have meaning. Both in the MDS context and in the more general context, this does occur often enough to make the use of the principal component directions useful to examine. However, the success rate for the INDSCAL axes appears to be far higher than for principal component directions.

A second comparison can be made with the techniques used in factor analysis to determine directions, such as varimax and its many relatives. Again, these work often enough to have value, but the INDSCAL axes seem to work better. No explanation is available for the differing success rates of these methods; INDSCAL does use three-way rather than two-way data, however, so the difference is reasonable.

JOSEPH B. KRUSKAL is a member of the Mathematics and Statistics Research Center of Bell Laboratories. He received his Ph.D. in mathematics from Princeton in 1954. He has taught at Columbia, Yale, and Cambridge among other universities, and has served as president of the Psychometric Society and the Classification Society. His research has ranged over a wide area, including mathematics, statistics, psychology, and linguistics. Dr. Kruskal is the author of numerous articles appearing in a variety of publications such as the Journal of Combinatorial Theory, Psychometrika, *the* Encyclopedia of Statistics, *and the* Journal of the Royal Statistical Society.

MYRON WISH is Research Head of the Interpersonal Communication Research Department of Bell Laboratories. He is also an Adjunct Professor of Psychology at Teachers College, Columbia University. Dr. Wish received his Ph.D. in psychology from the University of Michigan in 1966. His research has provided an excellent blend of multivariate methodology with social psychology. He is author of numerous articles, which have appeared in such publications as Journal of Personality and Social Psychology, Multivariate Behavioral Research, Handbook of Perception, *and* Contemporary Developments in Mathematical Psychology.

The two authors contributed equally to the
preparation of this work.